THE CUSTOMER-CENTRED STRATEGY

"This book covers important new ground on strategies to build strong customer relationships. An invaluable up-to-date guide on a subject of the highest priority for today's managers."

Peter Doyle, Professor of Marketing and Strategic Management, Warwick Business School

"Highly readable with well-chosen examples to illustrate the key messages and reinforced with excellent diagnostics and summary sections. The final part of the book provides readers with a kit bag of tools to enable them to apply the principles in their own organisations. A book on strategy written with the practitioner clearly in mind."

Ken Palframan, Human Resources Director, Chep Europe

The Institute of Management (IM) is at the
forefront of management development and
best management practice. The Institute
embraces all levels of management from
students to chief executives. It provides a
unique portfolio of services for all managers,
enabling them to develop skills and achieve
management excellence.

If you would like to hear more about the
benefits of membership, please write to
Department P, Institute of Management,
Cottingham Road, Corby NN17 1TT.

This series is commissioned by the
Institute of Management Foundation.

THE MILLENNIUM MANAGER

THE
CUSTOMER-CENTRED
STRATEGY

Thinking strategically about your customers

MARK JENKINS

the Institute of Management

FOUNDATION

PITMAN PUBLISHING

London · Hong Kong · Johannesburg
Melbourne · Singapore · Washington DC

PITMAN PUBLISHING
128 Long Acre, London WC2E 9AN
Tel: +44 (0)171 447 2000
Fax: +44 (0)171 240 5771

A Division of Pearson Professional Limited

First published in Great Britain 1997

ISBN 0 273 63004 0

British Library Cataloguing in Publication Data
A CIP catalogue record for this book can be obtained from the British Library

10 9 8 7 6 5 4 3 2 1

Typeset by Pantek Arts, Maidstone, Kent.
Printed and bound in Great Britain by Bell and Bain Ltd, Glasgow

The Publishers' policy is to use paper manufactured from sustainable forests.

ABOUT THE AUTHOR

Mark Jenkins is a senior lecturer in strategic management at Cranfield School of Management in the UK. Prior to joining Cranfield, he worked for the Lex Service Group and in the marketing and sales functions of Massey Ferguson Tractors Ltd, spending a number of years in the latter as an Area Sales Manager.

In his current role, he teaches on both the MBA and management short courses, specialising in the areas of competitive strategy, strategic capabilities and customer-facing organisations. His consulting activities reflect these teaching specialisations where he has worked throughout Europe, the USA and in parts of the Far East and Middle East. In addition to his work at Cranfield, he has contributed to programmes at Warwick Business School and the University of Colorado. He has published and presented a wide range of work in the areas of strategy and marketing, and is co-editor of the *Journal of Marketing Practice*.

Mark Jenkins BA, MSC, DPSE, PhD

ACKNOWLEDGEMENTS

Like most authors, I am indebted to the many groups and individuals who have been influential in the creation of this book, and, like those before me, I am unable to adequately acknowledge them all.

I am indebted to my colleagues at Cranfield School of Management and the many MBA and short-course students who have provided insights, advice and robust critique when it was required. The same is true of the organisations with whom I have worked as a consultant and the other universities and business schools where I have presented my ideas. However, there are four people whose ideas and concepts are featured in this book, and whose combination of academic rigour coupled with the desire for real practical relevance has been a significant contribution, both literally and spiritually, to this project. Cliff Bowman, Colin Eden, Gerry Johnson and Malcolm McDonald have all been, and continue to be, a source of inspiration for me.

Finally, I need to dedicate this book to the person who made sure that it was actually completed, Sandra, without whom I would probably still be working on the proposal, and to Anna and Beth for providing the many diversions which were sometimes welcome, but always total.

CONTENTS

FOREWORD

The Institute of Management's study *Management Development to the Millennium* confirmed that the demands on managers today are very different from those of ten, or even five, years ago. The demands of the new century will be even more different.

However managers should welcome the pressures that today's dynamic marketplace puts upon them – managing change to achieve something better is a principal, probably on-going task of management.

As the management world has become very much more complicated, a key skill is to be prepared for, and wherever possible predict, the changes that will occur in future. New technology, changing markets and changing organisational cultures are all crucially important influences on managers' behaviour and activities.

Technology is the key to combining the advantages of a very large organisation with the advantages of a very small one, while the competitive nature of the national and global marketplace means that total quality is becoming the minimum standard required to compete. Cultural changes however can never be forced. In a learning organisation there has to be a shift from dominant attention to short-term success towards creating a context that stimulates managers to experiment with opportunities in favour of long-term growth. Organisations must be dynamic – they have to change, both out of necessity and by choice. The manager's job of today therefore focuses more on action and less on analysis, with more emphasis on the intervention than on planning. These changes are happening in almost all organisations, both large and small, in both the private and public sectors. So whether you work for a giant multinational or a small local company, it is likely that you will have to change your way of working to keep up with the shifts in your market and benefit from the new opportunities of the new century.

I therefore unreservedly commend *The Millennium Manager* series both for its forward-looking approach and for continuing the debate around the direction of management and management development for UK plc.

Roger Young
Director General, Institute of Management

THE
MILLENNIUM
MANAGER

PRIORITY SKILLS FOR THE MANAGER OF 2001

In July 1995, the Institute of Management published a report, *Management Development to the Millennium,* based on interviews with opinion formers at the most senior managerial level of industry and commerce – all who had high expectations of their managers in their ability to lead and grow their organisations.

Managers are expected to have the ability to operate across a broad range of skills and competences. The *Management Development to the Millennium* report identified those skills and competencies that senior managers felt were essential for management and organisational success into the new millennium.

The following table from the report shows a list of the priority skills selected by respondents. Three-quarters of the managers surveyed indicated a clear focus on the 'harder' skills of strategic thinking and change management. Nevertheless, over four in ten endorsed the importance of facilitating others to contribute, in other words a classic 'softer' skill.

Skills for the manager in the next millennium

Base: 1,241 respondents	%
Strategic thinking, eg longer term, broader perspective, anticipating	78
Responding to and managing change	75
An orientation towards total quality/customer satisfaction	67
Financial management, eg role and impact of key financial indicators	46
Facilitating others to contribute	44
Understanding the role of information and IT	42
Verbal communication, eg coherent, persuasive	38
Organisational sensitivity, eg cross-functional understanding	37
Risk assessment in decision-making	35

This book addresses the indicated skill – *strategic thinking.* Other books in the **Pitman/IM Millennium Manager** series concentrate on some of the other skills listed above.

INTRODUCTION

This book has a single objective: to challenge and re-evaluate some of the assumptions which exist in organisations concerning the role of the customer in relation to strategy. It is not intended to provide a complete 'how to do it' package, but, rather, raise a series of questions about organisations which will allow those within them to redevelop and refine their thinking and actions.

In order to do this, the book is in three parts. The first part presents the argument or rationale as to why organisations should challenge the way they consider the customer, and why, at a strategic level, most are only paying lip-service to this issue.

The second part presents an iterative model which is designed to provide the tools and frameworks that are needed to explore the nature of customers and the way in which the organisation responds to them.

In the third and final part, we use integrating case studies to bring together some of the ideas and issues in an organisational context. Part 3 concludes with a review of the process and the issues it raises.

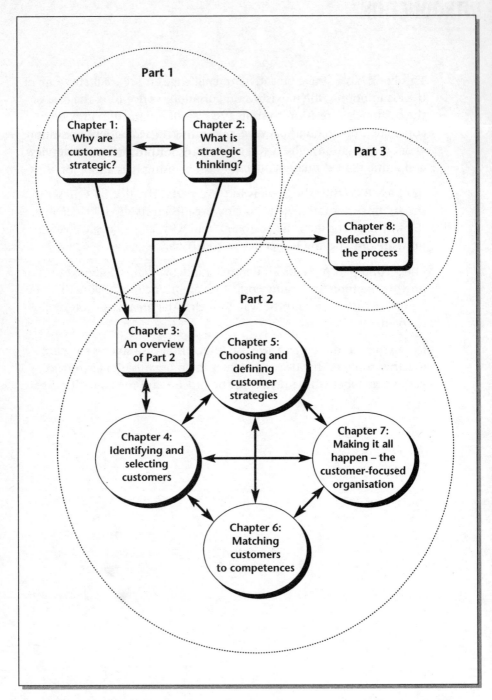

Figure I.1 Overview map of the structure of the book and how the issues relating to thinking strategically about customers connect

Figure I.1 is a map of the structure of the book and shows the relationships between the various chapters. We will be using such diagrams as guides in all the chapters in the book. This technique is based on the cognitive mapping approach developed by Colin Eden[1] and provides a way of organising issues and the causal relationships between them. As well as using it as a basis for providing an overview of the chapters in the book, we will also be using it as a tool for exploring issues in the scenario approach discussed in Chapter 4.

As can be seen in Figure I.1, Chapters 1 and 2 (Part 1) introduce and review the process, whereas Chapters 3, 4, 5, 6 and 7 (Part 2) provide an overview of the model which represents the process of thinking strategically about customers. Part 2 is not a prescriptive set of stages, it is a framework for strategic thinking than can help managers challenge some of their assumptions about the strategic task. In order to keep this as the central focus, each chapter includes a number of diagnostic frameworks, with examples, which you are encouraged to use. Finally, Chapter 8 and the Appendix make up Part 3. There we reflect on the process using some integrating case studies and present a series of pro forma to be used to apply some of the ideas in the book.

Each chapter begins with an overview map like that shown in Figure I.1 and concludes by identifying seven key summary points. These allow the reader to either reflect on the content of the chapter or read these first to decide whether or not it's worthwhile them reading the whole chapter. This is followed by a series of questions to help you incorporate the ideas of the chapter into your own organisation and, finally, a short diagnostic questionnaire, which allows those who feel more comfortable with numbers to evaluate their position regarding the concepts covered in the chapter.

However, the most important task is to make your own organisation the central case study in this book. To help you do this, pro forma for all the frameworks used in the book are available in the Appendix for your use. In this way your customer value will, hopefully, be maximised!

[1] Eden, C. (1992). 'On the Nature of Cognitive Maps', *Journal of Management Studies*, **29**, 3, 261–5.

KEY SUMMARY POINTS

1 The objective of this book is to rethink the way in which customers are incorporated into strategy.

2 This book aims to challenge you and focus on developing questions to be answered in your organisation – it is not about providing simplistic answers to these complicated issues.

3 The three parts of the book cover the rationale behind the book (Part 1), the model being developed to help strategic thinking about customers (Part 2) and reflections and case examples of the process (Part 3).

4 A mapping technique is used to introduce the chapters and explain the linkages between the various issues covered in them.

5 Each chapter concludes with a seven-point summary, like this one.

6 Each chapter also features a series of key questions and simple diagnostics to enable you to apply the concepts to your organisation.

7 In order for you to use these frameworks, a series of pro forma are included in the Appendix.

PART 1

THE RATIONALE
FOR THIS BOOK

CHAPTER

1

WHY ARE
CUSTOMERS
STRATEGIC?

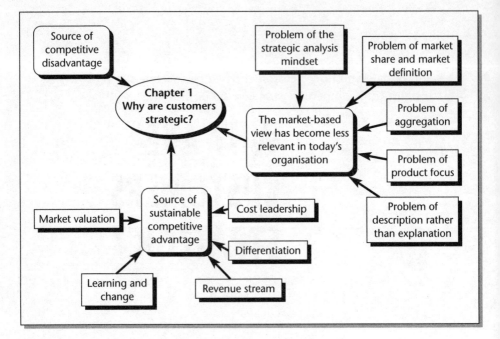

Figure 1.1 Overview map of the subjects covered in Chapter 1

Figure 1.1 shows the key elements in this chapter. First, we discuss why customers can be a source of both competitive advantage and competitive disadvantage. Second, we consider a number of issues which are making market-driven perspectives on strategy less appropriate and how a customer-based perspective can provide new insights into competitive strategy and positioning.

Customers are strategically important. This is one statement on which most managers, consultants and academics agree. A review of the annual reports of the organisations in the Fortune 500 or Financial Times 100 provides a wealth of references to customer focus, customer responsiveness and customer relationships. Each chairperson's statement implicitly claims that their organisation has somehow monopolised the concept of customer orientation and made it its own. Groups of managers will vigorously nod their heads when told that the future of their business depends on their customers. However, they will also smile and joke at how their organisation really deals with its customers. A senior manager with a large bank recalled how an important corporate client rang, wanting to speak with his account manager urgently. He was told that there was nobody available – they were all on a customer care course!

THE CUSTOMER PARADOX

That story illustrates the need for this book. At one level senior managers have no doubt about the importance of customers, but the paradox is that this is so 'global' that it prohibits them from turning these broad motherhood statements into a reality in the day-to-day running of the organisation. This book is intended to provide a bridge between the broad statements of strategic intent and the point at which the strategy is delivered: the interface between the organisation and its customers. In order to do this, we start by considering three aspects of the customer paradox. First, we re-examine why it is that customers should be considered central to the strategic thinking of the organisation. This issue is often taken for granted and rarely examined in detail. Second, we consider why, in reality, the more widely used frameworks for strategic thinking do not start with, and thereby do not fully enhance, the relationship with customers. Third, we look at how strategic thinking can be developed in order to ensure that strategies are being driven by customer-based issues.

WHY ARE CUSTOMERS STRATEGICALLY IMPORTANT?

In considering this question there are five areas in which customers contribute to the development of the business:

- the revenue stream
- market valuation
- sustained competitive advantage
- as a catalyst for learning and change.

Revenue stream

Perhaps the most common definition of 'customers', is that these are individuals or businesses who provide revenue for your business. As the revenue stream is sourced from customers, this makes them potentially the most important strategic stakeholders. Indeed, the question 'Who pays your wages?' is often used to try and redirect employees' attention towards its customers.

There are a number of dimensions to the revenue stream through which customers can strongly influence the financial balance of the organisation. The amount of revenue growth is driven by increased expenditure by customers, although there may be major implications as to whether or not this is because the same customers are buying more or more customers are buying the same amount (this is explored in Chapter 5). The volatility of revenue levels is driven by customer demand, whether this be on an annual basis, reflecting seasonal variations, or over longer periods, reflecting business cycles or other factors. Understanding these issues requires an understanding of customers and the nature of their situations. For example, a truck rental company receives revenue streams when customers unexpectedly need to increase their transport capacity. In this case, revenue streams are intermittent and, while profitability is extremely good, cash flow places a significant constraint on the development of the business. An understanding of driving forces such as these, which create a situation in which demand is suddenly likely to rise, help the business anticipate changes in revenue flows more effectively.

The term revenue stream is used deliberately to distinguish it from product sales. Increasingly, the product is becoming secondary to the process of the relationship between a supplier and its customers. For examples, in the drive towards remanufacturing and reverse logistics, organisations such as Kodak and Rank Xerox are reclaiming product components from their customers and incorporating these into new product forms. This makes the distinction between 'whole goods' and parts less important, but, most of all, it emphasises a shift away from discreet products with set lifetimes and towards establishing a revenue flow between customers and suppliers in exchange for the capability to satisfy specific needs, such as photography or photocopying.

Many companies fail not because they are unprofitable, but because they run out of cash. Kaplan and Norton[1] in their work on the Balanced Scorecard, note how the performance of one company in achieving project management deadlines had close links (not surprisingly) with the speed with which customers paid their accounts and, therefore, the amount of resources that were tied up in accounts receivable. Cash flow is not just something which occurs in the finance department, it is a result of the way we do business with our customers.

Figure 1.2 illustrates this point. Moving from left to right, the speed with which customers pay can have either a negative or positive impact on an organisation's cash flow. The issue in a competitive context is that if your customers pay more quickly than do your competitors' customers, then you have relatively more financial resources than they do which you can use in building a competitive advantage.

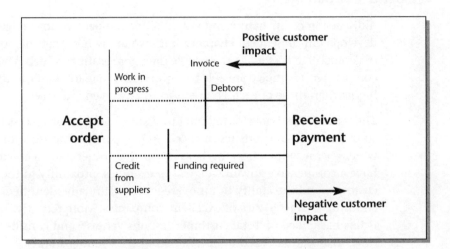

Figure 1.2 Considering the potential influence of customers on cash flow

Market valuation

Customers are not only strategic stakeholders in terms of delivering revenue streams, they are also a strategic asset which can enhance market (stock) valuation. While there has been a great deal of discussion of brand valuation in management accounts,[2] there is no disguising the fact that organisations create equity value through their relationships with customers. This creates value for shareholders and can also create a barrier to prevent predators from acquiring companies solely for the tangible assets. However, it can also make companies that achieve such value particularly attractive to other companies that are seeking to build industry presence. For example, the European food industry has seen a spate of mergers and acquisitions. Organisations such as Unilever, Danone and Nestlé have paid significant premiums for organisations because of their 'brand' value.[3]

Brand value is the relationship of an organisation with its consumers or final customers. Brands cannot exist in isolation. They exist because they are valued by customers. You cannot create or sustain or brand value without starting with customers. A pasta brand, such as La Familia in Spain or Birkel in Germany, has a high value in its home market. However, if you pick these companies up and move them to the UK, the value reduces to the tangible assets of the business. The assumption that the brand has a life of its own is therefore erroneous – brands and brand values are only created and sustained because of their acceptance by customers.

Competitive advantage

A discussion of the nature and potential for competitive advantage is developed in subsequent chapters, but save to say here that the notion of competitive advantage is a simple one: organisations which have competitive advantage are able to earn returns that are significantly higher than those of their competitors in any given industry.[4]

The 'Excellence' books[5] attempted to distil the nature of success by studying the characteristics of excellent companies (that is, companies which, because they have higher returns than others, are deemed to have a competitive advantage). In these studies, proximity to the customer and the ability to innovate were continually identified as enduring characteristics of excellent companies. More recently, Tom Peters has talked of 'total customer responsiveness'[6] and considers how organisations need to become obsessive about customer satisfaction in order to achieve excellence.

Competitive advantage by means of differentiation

In Michael Porter's work on generic strategies,[7] the need to create a product or service which is seen by the customer to be different is central to differentiated and focused differentiated strategies for competitive advantage. The basis of differentiation is that, from the customers' perspective, your product or service does hold this extra differentiated value. Organisations that can create a product or service which is seen, by customers, to be different from those of the competition have, in effect, created a monopoly situation. Customers are prepared to pay a premium because they perceive there to be no direct competition. This premium translates into a higher return on capital for the organisation, provided that the costs of the differentiation are not significantly greater than the costs of competitors' products to them. Hence the high returns which have been sustained by means of differentiation by 'brand builders' such as Coca-Cola and British Airways

Competitive advantage by means of cost leadership

There is also evidence that customers can provide a cost advantage as well as a revenue advantage. Reicheld and Sasser[8] illustrated the potential cost advantages of higher customer retention levels empirically. New customers are far more costly to serve than existing customers. This is due to the higher initial set-up cost and because existing customers are able to solve their own problems more effectively than new ones.

These mechanisms have been shown to apply to many different industries. For example, in insurance, the cost of underwriting a new policy is roughly twice the percentage of sales for a renewal policy, so if a company is able to improve the proportion of repeat customers, its total costs will shrink dramatically. The same applies to software. Whereas helpline demand for new customers is very high, existing customers place virtually no demands on this service – even for upgrades the requirement for such assistance is still very low. From this principle we can create a typical cost profile, as illustrated in Figure 1.3.

The proportions of these different types of customers may therefore have a significant impact on the cost structure of a business.

Another way in which customers can create cost savings is by participating in the creation of your product and service. Most parents will know only too well how frustrating it is when faced with the 'simple' instructions for their child's castle, train set or other toy they

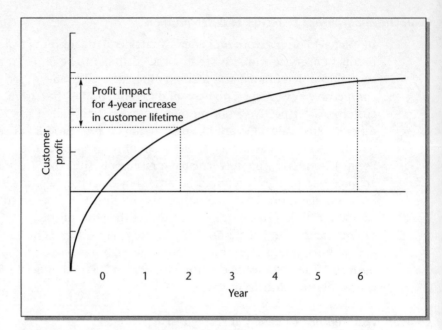

Figure 1.3 Customer profitability over time
Source: Based on Reicheld[9]

have received at Christmas or for their birthday, to find that having assumed that the construction of the toy will take just a few minutes, you end up spending several hours on what seems like a major civil engineering project! In these situations we, as customers, are participating in the construction of the product. We are creating the final result, and it is only because we are able to and accept to undertake this role that the cost of this process is absorbed by customers.

Many breakthroughs in service industries have arisen because customers have been educated and prepared to undertake new tasks as part of the service process. For example, in catalogue-based stores, such as Argos, customers select their products, pay for them at one desk and then go to the warehouse counter to collect them. In more traditional stores, all of these activities would be undertaken by the assistants, but because Argos pass these activities back to customers, it is able to handle greater volumes of business at lower relative cost. The success of the Swedish retailer Ikea is also based on this type of philosophy. Using quality materials and unique designs from a large number of specialist suppliers, Ikea requires its customers to be adept in road haulage and furniture assembly in order to make the concept work.

Customers can do more than lower costs by participating in your routine operations, however. Eric von Hippel at MIT has, for some time, argued that more cost-effective research and development (R&D) can be delivered by harnessing key customers in the development of new products or services.[10] Customers who are at the leading edge of their field are often able to solve their own problems, thereby creating enhanced products or services. In this way, they are often able to develop concepts into viable prototypes, which is typically the most expensive phase in the R&D process. If this knowledge is captured by organisations it can therefore significantly reduce R&D costs. Von Hippel notes that to achieve this there has to be a shift from 'manufacturer-active' R&D, where the organisation plays the active role, to 'customer-active' R&D, with the customer driving the process and developing solutions to their own problems. Here is an example of this. In the 1950s, guitar player Les Paul, fed up with being drowned out by louder brass instruments and percussion, used a simple microphone pick-up, amplifier and speaker to increase the volume of his guitar, allowing him to compete with his colleagues' more resonant instruments. His solution created a new product form – the electric guitar. The guitar manufacturer Gibson was then able to successfully launch this new product, aptly named the Gibson Les Paul.

The basis of von Hippel's argument rests on companies identifying those customers who are most innovative and likely to come up with innovative and successful solutions. Other examples of such customers include top salons introducing protein-based shampoos by adding an egg to conventional shampoo to give it more body, and the farmer who created a high-productivity 6-metre- (6½-yard-) wide seed drill by welding together two 3-metre- (3¼-yard-)wide drills.

Sustainable competitive advantage

One of the most powerful impacts of the 'Excellence' books was to vividly illustrate how success is rarely sustainable. By 1990, more than 50 per cent of the companies featured in the original study were either bankrupt, acquired via a hostile takeover or underperforming. While many used this as a reason for dismissing the validity of the study, others realised that the real issue was not excellence *per se*, but the sustainability of excellence in corporate environments which are uncertain and highly dynamic. The rules of the game and the structures of industries are undergoing continual rapid change.

Customers can play a vital role in providing a basis for *sustaining* advantage. Whereas advantage lies in having something different to the competition, sustainability comes about when you have something different which is very difficult for competitors to imitate or substitute. While it may be possible to protect some aspects of a product to deliver sustainability (such as the Polaroid process) legally, it is more likely that sustainability is created via something which is highly complicated and intangible. It is therefore difficult to define and imitate. The variability and complexity of customers, combined with the variability and complexity of the supplying organisation, make customer relationships one of the most difficult areas to manage, but also one of the most difficult to copy.

One example of an organisation which has shown sustainable returns well in excess of the industry average is British Airways. The average return for the airline industry in 1995 was 0.5 per cent,[11] whereas BA made a return well in excess of 10 per cent. Sir Colin Marshall, CEO, made the following observation to illustrate the role of customers in sustaining competitive advantage:

● ● ●

Anyone can run an airline, but very few can serve people [that is, customers] to a high standard. Because it's a competence which is hard to build it's very difficult for competitors to imitate.
Sir Colin Marshall, 1996[12]

● ● ●

In retailing, the sustained advantage achieved by stores such as Marks & Spencer in the UK and Nordstrom in the US is not only impressive, but it is virtually impossible to replicate. This sustainability is created by the organisational culture and is embedded in the way it relates to its customers (we shall discuss these issues in more detail in Chapters 6 and 7).

Learning and change

Much has been written on the topic of learning – learning from competitors, learning from employees and so on. In this context, learning from customers is perhaps the most important source of learning and catalyst for change that an organisation can have.

Customers are a significant source of learning because they have a perspective which is based on meeting their needs and solving their problems. They can identify when we're no longer in touch with their needs and thereby be a catalyst for change. Creating a dialogue with customers is fundamental to understanding where the opportunities for sustainable competitive advantage exist and, most importantly, what needs to be done in the organisation to realise this.

While Hamel and Prahalad rightly point out that customer satisfaction *now* is not the basis for competitive advantage in the *future*,[13] the right customers can be challenging and thought provoking in the issues they raise with an organisation. No organisation can be all things to all customers, but it needs to understand who the strategically important customers are, the revenue streams of the future.

The reason for our existence

So far, the discussion has implicitly assumed that we are dealing with organisations that have as their central focus the achievement of sustained profit. This is not so in the case of public-sector organisations or charities as their purpose for existing is based on the serving of particular groups of customers. In these cases, the concept of the customer group is one on which the whole organisation is based, but defining that group can be highly problematical. Is the customer of a police force the government or the public at large? Differing interpretations of customer definitions are not just semantic, they are indicative of the priorities and values of the individuals within the organisation. We need, therefore, to understand these definitions and their significance in the workings of the organisation.

In not-for-profit contexts, the term 'customer' is often pejorative in that it implies an economic transaction, which is often inappropriate. Should a school or hospital have customers? This is not an issue which can be answered here, but the purpose of this book is to discuss how particularly important stakeholder groups (which I refer to as customers, but other terms, as we have seen, may be appropriate for your organisation) can be brought into the strategic thinking of the organisation. It is not intended to undermine many of those values that have made many public service organisations so effective, but it is intended to challenge and clarify exactly who should be the focus of organisational activity and where this activity can be made more effective and efficient.

The five areas we have looked at are of undoubted strategic importance. All of them underpin sustained profit performance, shareholder value and organisational effectiveness. However, it is important to know, too, that having identified these clear benefits which customers provide, not all customers provide such benefits – in fact, customers can be dangerous.

WHY ARE CUSTOMERS DANGEROUS?

Customers are dangerous for a number of reasons:

- they may cost more to serve than we realise
- they may not be able to tell us what they want
- even worse, they may tell us one thing but behave in a totally contradictory manner.

Let us look at these in more detail. Customers can be costly. For example, those of us who pay off our credit cards every month are dangerous. We cost the credit card companies more than they make on us – in fact, we are effectively subsidised by those who do not clear their account every month. If a new entrant in the credit card business is able to secure a higher proportion of high credit customers, they will have a profit advantage over the competition.

In my view, the customer survey can be a highly overrated and misused management tool. It is assumed that if you ask customers a question, they will be able and willing to provide an answer which reflects the way they behave. Most market research professionals know this to be a nonsense. Customers often do not know how they will behave if a certain series of cues are provided or they provide answers which are more about creating acceptance with their peers than providing accurate information. For example, the beer consumption of the UK would increase by more than ten times, as would the sales of condoms, if the younger male respondents of questionnaires are to be believed. One of the more famous cases of the danger of believing what customers tell you is the Ford Edsel. Having discovered market research, Ford set out to build a car based on what everyone wanted. Having undertaken extensive research to identify what everyone would like to see in a car, Ford created the car which everyone said they would like, but in reality nobody actually bought it. In his book on the advertising industry, David Ogilvy recounted the fortuitous decision he made not to compete for the Edsel account.[14] The point is not that customers deliberately mislead, but that what they say and what they do often have two distinctly different outcomes.

In the same way that customers can create competitive advantage, they can also create competitive disadvantage.

What is perhaps more important in a competitive context is that if one organisation does not focus on specific groups of customers, then it will not suffer a competitive disadvantage, as long as all its competitiors are applying an equal lack of focus. However, if some competitors begin to focus on those customers who are likely to see more value in the products or services being offered and who are also less costly to serve, then the competitive disadvantage occurs. If competitors are building stronger relationships with the most profitable types of customers, then any amount of buying of market share will fail to generate the same level of potential earnings.

We have therefore summarised some of the main reasons why customers need to be considered at the strategic level of business. However, it is my belief that, despite the fundamental role customers play in the strategic success of businesses, there is much that can be done to improve the way customers feature in the strategic thinking of organisations.

CUSTOMERS IN THE TRADITIONAL STRATEGY PROCESS

So far little has been raised which could be considered contentious. We can all agree that customers are strategically important without too much argument. However, when we start to consider how strategy happens in organisations, customers rarely occupy a central location in this process. An audit of most strategy texts and MBA syllabuses will show that there are dominant frameworks which are applied to aid strategic thinking. These would include basic concepts, such as product and industry lifecycles, the Boston Consulting Group portfolio matrix or BCG grid (who hasn't heard of cash cows and stars), and others, such as the Ansoff matrix for product/market growth and the directional policy matrix (or GE grid) for aligning organisational strengths to particular markets.[15]

All of these are useful and established frameworks. However, they all have one major drawback in terms of optimising the strategic thinking in an organisation: they focus on *markets* rather than *customers*. A focus on markets means that they do not provide the clarity of strategic thinking which we need in order to integrate customers into the process.

A number of problems exist with frameworks which consider markets rather than customers. These can be summarised as being:

- the problem of market share and market definition
- the problem of aggregation
- the problem of product focus
- the problem of description rather than explanation
- the problem of strategic analysis mindset.

Let us now look at each of these problems in turn.

The problem of market share and market definition

One of the basic principles of the market share approach to competitive strategy is that market share directly increases profitability because of a variety of cost savings that can be derived from economies of scale and economies of experience. The relationship between market share and profitability is outlined in Figure 1.4. This is drawn from the PIMS studies which were undertaken in the 1970s to attempt to determine which variables explained variation in the return on investment (ROI) of a variety of organisations.

It seems to be taken for granted in many organisations that market share is a good thing and is the basis on which the prosperity of the organisation can be built. However, there are several assumptions on which these conclusions are based. First, that market share is the cause of increased profitability. While the PIMS database has shown a correlation between market share and ROI, correlation is a measure of association rather than causality. The data therefore show that where market share is positive, ROI is also likely to be positive, in the same way that people who have large feet are also likely to have large hands. However, a further leap of faith is needed to reach the

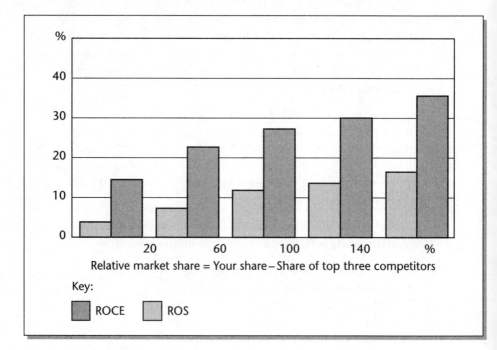

Relative market share = Your share – Share of top three competitors

Key:

■ ROCE   ▫ ROS

Figure 1.4 The relationship between market share and profitability

Source: PIMS database

conclusion that increases in market share cause increases in profitability, in the same way that increasing the size of our hands will increase the size of our feet. In fact, a study which re-examined the PIMS data[16] concluded that most of the association between market share and ROI is spurious and is likely to be the joint outcome of a third variable. In the case of the anatomical analogy, this may be that individuals have large feet and large hands because they are tall. In the same way, an organisation which is well managed with motivated staff may have a high market share and a high ROI, but it is problematical to assume that it is the high market share which creates its high ROI.[17]

The second issue is the assumption that all markets can be easily and unequivocally defined. For example, the non-alcoholic drink Aqua-Libra, launched by International Distillers and Vintners in the early 1990s, could claim to have secured almost 80 per cent of the market in the first year of sales. This would be an impressive message to investors, no doubt, all of whom would be seeing how profitable this product was going to become once plotted on the Boston Consulting Group (BCG) grid. But how is this share arrived at?

The market can be calculated, not untypically, in a way which is defined by product specification. As a non-alcoholic drink which was not a fruit juice, Aqua-Libra's market can be defined as herbal drinks. Here it competes with such heady delights as concentrated carrot juice and would be, far and away, the market leader. The importance of this example is that any product or business can be on the left (most desirable) side of the BCG grid, it just depends how we define the market. Had the market been defined as a non-alcoholic adult drink, competing with non-alcoholic wine, mineral water, fruit juice and so on, then the market share would be closer to 0.8 than 80 per cent. As we can see in Figure 1.5, we get some very different answers from the BCG matrix depending on which market definition we use. In the case of A^1, we use the definition of herbal drinks. Here, the product has a dominant market position in a category which is growing rapidly due to the launch of a new non-alcoholic adult drink. In the case of A^2, the market is redefined to include all soft drinks. This market is relatively more mature and, therefore, the rate of growth is reducing. However, this is also compounded by a significant drop in relative market share as a whole new cluster of competitors is incorporated into this definition. Finally, A^3 shows the market defined as the overall drinks market. At this level, the growth rate is very low and the relative market share is minute. The question remains as to which definition should be used?

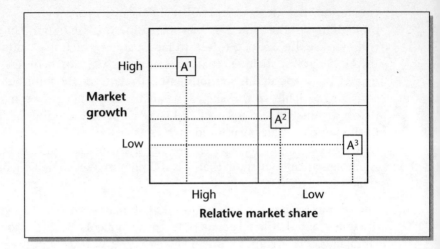

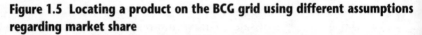

Figure 1.5 Locating a product on the BCG grid using different assumptions regarding market share

The issue of market definition can be developed at two levels. The first is the demand side of the market. If customers are using a product such as Aqua-Libra, what other products would they see as being alternatives to it? In economic terms, these are the products with a high cross-elasticity of demand. If the new drink is increased in price, the demand for these products will increase. The demand side definition would probably consider most soft drinks and mineral water to be competitors, locating the product at A^2. The logic that market share is the driver for profitability is that market share creates economies of scale and experience which will be greater than they are for the competition, thereby providing a competitive advantage.

The second level is therefore concerned with the supply side of market definition, as these savings are only to be found where the economies can be achieved. Let us assume that there are four major cost elements to the production and distribution of a non-alcoholic drink such as Aqua-Libra. These are new product development (continually developing new product formulations), production (putting the liquid in the bottle), distribution/logistics (managing the supply chain) and marketing (developing the brand franchise with the consumer).

If these are the four basic elements of cost, then the market definition question concerns whether or not these types of processes are common to all players in the drinks market (A^3), are specific to the herbal drinks sector (A^1) or involve some combination in between.

This suggests that, in order to clarify where advantage can be achieved by means of market share economies, a different, supply-driven market definition needs to be used. The suggestion here is that these economies are far more likely to be achieved across the whole of the drinks market rather than in one particular sector of it. The competences needed to compete in the herbal drinks sector are relatively common to those needed to compete in the whole of the drinks market. Therefore, the dominant players can only be those who apply these competences across different sectors, rather than those which choose particular niches.

However, this level of definition may not explain who you are competing with in terms of the choices which consumers make among competing products. The problem therefore, is that, in order to understand the competitive situation and to explore where the basis of competitive advantage may lie, we have to consider multiple rather than single market definitions.

The problem of market definition is compounded if we look to the future. What about new, innovative products, how do they fit in? The problem with innovations is that they often redefine market boundaries. The notion of gap analysis is that innovations can be based on the gap between two markets. For example, Audi successfully brought together two market segments in the car market with the performance car and estate car (note that these are product-driven definitions of market segments), while Reliant had done this in the 1970s with their Scimitar model. This segment has undergone a revival in the mid 1990s with entrants such as BMW and Volvo. In the financial products market, the plastic card has been combined with a current account to create the debit card. In the drinks market, soft drinks, such as lemonade, have been combined with alcoholic drinks to create alcopops. All of these innovations are based on product or service definitions, but they are fundamentally incremental changes – they still satisfy the same customer needs of the same customers, but in a slightly enhanced way. Many of these innovations are driven not by clearly enhanced customer value or price, but by the desire to continually stay ahead of or keep up with the competition.

However, with this continual process of innovation comes an inevitable drift away from the original product-dominated market definition. Thus, retailers use financial services to create buyer loyalty and car manufacturers and computer manufacturers, in offering new ways of acquiring the use of leading-edge products, are transforming financial services. The current Apple computer is able to show TV programmes in addition to multitasking on graphics packages, games or word processing. Is cable TV a separate market to entertainment, to software development, to cinema? Is management consulting a separate market to computer applications support, to business education, to on-line business publishing? Increasingly, market definitions are becoming obtuse, if not irrelevant to understanding where the future revenue streams of the organisation will come from. There is much to suggest that such revenue streams are created and sustained via customer relationships, customers who may use and acquire many different products and services, in many different contexts, but who are the common thread between these multiple activities and transactions.

This is the background to the trend towards 'fuzzy' market boundaries. At one time, markets such as financial services and computing were clearly defined by their distinct products or services. However, now, we appear to be moving towards a situation where markets do not have boundaries but are viewed in infinite space. A firm's activities may overlap many markets, so the market framework is becoming less relevant to understanding how our business is operating.

I recently supervised strategy project undertaken by a group of MBAs. The team was engaged in a strategy review for an engineering test centre based in the UK. At first glance, its market definition is straightforward – testing facilities and volume of business. However, the more the members of the group talked to potential customers, the more they realised that the real value in the customers' eyes was that the test centre was providing expertise and consulting services, particularly in the area of new product development. This perspective provided far more clarity in understanding sustainable competitive advantage, but also illustrated that this market was very unclear, with the facilities part of the service offer being provided, in part, by other testing services, in-house testing services, but the more attractive consulting services being provided by management consultants and specialist technology consultants.

As market boundaries are becoming continuous, rather than discrete, the market is rapidly becoming almost impossible to define. Customers, however, *can* be defined, and it is from their perspective that more clarity can be achieved in our strategic thinking.

The problem of aggregation

The advantage of markets is that they give us some certainty in our strategic thinking. Their simplicity doesn't ask awkward questions about our strategic assumptions concerning the potential for complicated channels to market (that is, differing groups of customers) or for the potentially huge variation in customer requirements. Terms such as 'automotive', 'healthcare', 'pharmaceuticals' and 'industrial' are wonderfully concise and reassuringly familiar. However, they may mask huge differences in buying approaches and, most importantly, variations in the opportunities for competitive advantage. It can be argued that this concern can be remedied by splitting up the market into market segments. However, this process in itself rarely provides the detailed insights needed to explore the opportunities for competitive advantage.

The essence of Michael Porter's 'focus' strategy or the 'niche' strategies[18] referred to in the marketing literature is that some unique pocket of customer demand has been matched to particular organisational capabilities. These pockets of demand are rarely illuminated by the aggregate concept of the market. The market (and even its segments) is obvious to all and therefore does not help explore potential sources of advantage. For example, Chep is a global multimillion-pound business which is highly profitable and enjoys relatively high barriers to entry. Its market is difficult to define (see previous section), but could be assumed to be part of the logistics market. However, its business of pooling pallets, which involves highly sophisticated asset management, meets quite different needs and operates in a wholly different way to logistics operations such as Exel Logistics, yet, at a strategic analysis level, both companies could be considered to be in the same market.

The problem of product focus

A 'market' is where products or services and customers come together. However, because we understand and can measure products and services more easily than customers, our view of the market inevitably becomes a product-led concept. The danger of using markets for strategic thinking is that, inevitably, they focus our attention on products or services rather than customers. In many marketing texts, a distinction is drawn between a product orientation (we sell what we make) and a market orientation (we make what we can sell). It seems, however, that often a focus on the market is nothing more than a product orientation with some customer demographics thrown in. Of course, products and services are important, but, for the reasons outlined earlier, they do not provide us with the basis for achieving a sustainable advantage – this can only come from an insight into how customers see and value the product or service.

A product-focused approach to defining, segmenting and understanding markets offers a distinct contrast to one which focuses on customers' demands. A product-focused approach assumes that future returns are based on selling more products, and market segmentation is often concerned with classifying different types of products sold, rather than understanding variations in consumer demand. A product-focused approach does not anticipate new forms of products which can satisfy customers' needs, so it is not strategic. Such an approach has been most notable in the computer market, where demand has switched from products (PCs) to complete solutions (software, PC and service support). This has led many companies to rethink the traditional, product-based distinction of hardware and software and to consider integrating these to satisfy customers' demand.

The problem of description rather than explanation

A market is the output of the relationship between a firm and its customers. We need markets and we need to understand markets. Markets give a sense of proportion and historical data on the patterns of demand. However, markets are essentially descriptions of what has happened. They show us what happens *after* the strategy. Markets do not help us to understand where the potential sources of sustained competitive advantage may be. If this is our central strategic question, we have to be thinking more widely than markets.

For example, Figure 1.5 shows the fight between the VW Golf and Vauxhall Astra for a share of the European small car market. The first point is that it illustrates where decline has occurred and makes assumptions about where growth may occur in the future. It does not help us to understand the background to points where advantage may be found, either in terms of differential or cost advantage. Neither does it tell us about how and where such products may be bought and supported in the future. To do this, we need to go deeper – we need to have a clear understanding of the nature and dynamics of the customer side of the market in order to effectively consider and define strategy.

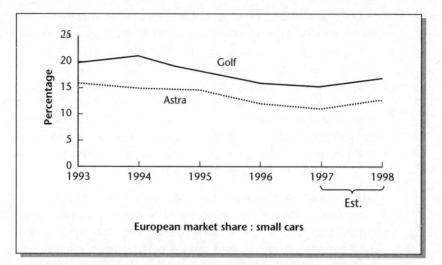

Figure 1.6 A tough race: comparing the VW Golf and Vauxhall Astra

Source: Reprinted from March 10, 1997 issue of *Business Week* by special permission; © 1997 by the McGraw-Hill Companies, Inc.[19]

The problem of strategic analysis mindset

The growth of the strategy consulting industry and the numbers of managers who hold MBAs means that the basic strategy concepts are widely accepted and understood. This is fine, and as a management educator I can only be happy with this situation. However, if we all use the same frameworks and apply the same thinking, where is the basis for competitive advantage? You may have heard the story of the Japanese companies exploiting their Western competitors' obsession with market share. By temporarily reducing their competitors' share they create a situation where competition withdraws from the market, as most of the strategy matrices indicate that high returns will only be forthcoming where a high market share is achieved. Industries have generic markets and segments, which tend to cause a convergence of competitive strategies, everyone playing the same game. However, many strategic breakthroughs have been created by organisations which break with the accepted view of the market and its needs and redefine the business. This redefinition has to centre on the needs (expressed or potential) of customers. If they do not, the innovation fails and the industry recipe[20] strengthens itself as the only way to succeed in this market. Where they succeed, the recipe is either redefined or held together by other non-competitive means, such as government intervention or regulation.

All of the above emphasises entrepreneurial approaches to strategy. Entrepreneurship can, therefore, provide the basis for advantage, by redefining the rules, applying the rules of one industry to another, reformulating organisations, services and, most specifically, providing customers with new sources of value. Entrepreneurship does not come from never-ending market analysis, but it does come from creative thinking and the generation of new insights about customers. Entrepreneurs have often been shown to hold an intuitive grasp of their customers' needs. In this regard, market analysis does not help us to become entrepreneurial.

All of the above problems point to a core issue: ultimately, each customer makes an individual (or in business to business, collective) decision as to whether or not to use a particular supplier. Unless we take a customer rather than market perspective, we fail to ask important, detailed questions about the way in which these decisions are made and, therefore, the way in which advantage can be generated and sustained. The argument is that we do not sufficiently represent customers in the strategy process. The central reason for this is that the majority of frameworks applied in the analysis of a firm's environment are concerned with markets rather than customers. This seems a rather petty, semantic distinction, but, this is a key issue as it means that customers are precluded from the strategic thinking which is taking place in the organisation. Markets, as noted by Tom Peters,[21] do not buy products or services, customers do. If this line of argument is followed through, markets do not offer revenue streams, enhance market valuation, create differential, cost or sustained advantage and create opportunities for learning and change, but customer relationships do.

THINKING STRATEGICALLY ABOUT CUSTOMERS

If we accept that strategic thinking needs to start with customers rather than markets, then there are already various frameworks which encourage this perspective. Bowman and Faulkner's[22] customer matrix considers competitive strategy from the customers' point of view; Parasuraman, et al.'s SERVQUAL model[23] considers how the service gaps should be managed to maximise customers' expectations and satisfaction. Brand mapping[24] is also used in many texts as a way of positioning products in competitive space as visualised by customers. These are important frameworks and ones which complement the existing market-based frameworks.

The problem, in terms of developing strategic thinking, is that the market perspective provides clarity and simplicity, but this is at an aggregate level which does not allow us to determine the real basis for competitive advantage. In contrast, the customer-based models provide us with a customer-driven perspective, but require that they be operationalised at the level of individual customers in order for them to be meaningful. This paradox is not unfamiliar to the strategy debate, where broad issues and big pictures have to be considered in terms of specific responsibilities, actions and outcomes in order to make them happen.

The position of this text is that managers require a process which enables them to create the detail and reality of the customers' perspective, but, at the same, time allows them to deal with broad issues and the cohesive strategic direction of the organisation. Not an easy task, but one which, it is hoped, will be aided by the following ideas which are designed to create a map to allow strategic thinking to balance these two critical areas.

KEY SUMMARY POINTS

1 There are few organisations today who are not espousing customer values and a customer-focused strategy.

2 The customer paradox is that it is very easy to espouse customer values, but very difficult to deliver these right through the organisation.

3 A strategy is only realised when it is delivered to customers. Therefore, it needs to be constructed around customers.

4 Customers contribute to the business in five key areas: revenue streams, market valuation, sustained competitive advantage, as a catalyst for learning and change and as the basis for the existence of the organisation.

5 But customers are also dangerous and can have a negative effect on the performance of the business if you have the wrong ones.

6 The traditional strategy process is based on the assumption that the market is the most important level at which to consider competitive strategy. There are several problems associated with this. These are summarised as being the problem of market share and market definition, the problem of aggregation, the problem

of product focus, the problem of description rather than explanation and the problem of the strategic analysis mindset.

7 The advantage of basing strategy on customers, rather than the market is that this enables us to see more clearly where the basis for a sustained competitive advantage lies.

KEY QUESTIONS AND DIAGNOSTICS

Can you identify those customers who are a strategic advantage, and those who are a strategic liability?

How much of what you do is based on the concept of markets and market share. What would the implications be of switching to focusing on specific groups of customers and developing the business with them?

How many different market definitions may exist for your organisation and how do you perform at these different levels?

STRATEGIC THINKING DIAGNOSTIC

Score each of these statements in terms of how strongly you agree or disagree with them. Add up the scores and see what your total means.

	Agree		Disagree		
In our organisation, market share is the basis of all our activity.	1	2	3	4	5
While we do not have a lot of details about particular types of customers, we can plot market share almost daily and to a very fine level of detail.	1	2	3	4	5
The basis of our competitive advantage is to achieve a high level of market share.	1	2	3	4	5
We rarely consider the costs of serving different customers.	1	2	3	4	5
We know exactly which customers are an asset and which ones are a liability.	1	2	3	4	5
We do not mind losing customers so long as we gain market share overall.	1	2	3	4	5
We have a very clear, measurable definition of our market.	1	2	3	4	5

Score

25–35: You have surfaced a number of concerns which the ideas in this book are intended to deal with.

15–25: Stuck in the middle – read on and see if this moves your score upwards.

0–15: Heavy emphasis on the market-driven approach – read on and see if this changes.

REFERENCES

[1] Kaplan, R. S., and Norton, D. P. (1996) *The Balanced Scorecard*, Boston, MA, Harvard Business School Press

[2] See, for example, Chapter 6 in Doyle, P. (1994), *Marketing Management and Strategy*, Hemel Hempstead, Prentice-Hall

[3] Verity, J. (1995), *The European Food Industry*, Cranfield, Beds, Cranfield School of Management

[4] Porter, M. (1985), *Competitive Advantage*, New York, Free Press

[5] For example, Peters, T., and Waterman, R. (1982), *In Search of Excellence*, New York, Harper & Row

[6] Peters, T. (1988), *Thriving on Chaos*, London, Macmillan

[7] Porter, M. (1980), *Competitive Strategy*, New York, Free Press

[8] Reichheld, F. F., and Sasser, W. E., Jr. (1990), 'Zero Defections: Quality Comes to Services', *Harvard Business Review*, 68 (September/October) 105–11

[9] Reichheld, F. F. (1996), *The Loyalty Effect*, Boston, MA, Harvard Business School Press

[10] Von Hippel, E. (1978), 'Successful Industrial Products from Customer Ideas' *Journal of Marketing*, January, 39–49

[11] Fortune's Global 500, *Fortune Magazine*, August 7, 1995

[12] Prokesch, S. E. (1995), 'Competing on Customer Service: An Interview with British Airways' Sir Colin Marshall', *Harvard Business Review*, November–December, 101–12

[13] Hamel, G., and Prahalad, C. K. (1994), *Competing for the Future*, Boston, MA, Harvard Business School Press

[14] Ogilvy, D. (1963), *Confessions of an Advertising Man*, New York, Atheneum

[15] For example, see Steiner, G. (1979), *Strategic Planning*, New York, Free Press, or Kotler, P. (1991), *Marketing Management*, Englewood Cliffs, Prentice-Hall, for this type of approach

[16] Jacobson, R., and Aaker, D. A. (1985), 'Is market share all that it's cracked up to be?', *Journal of Marketing*, 49, Fall, 11–22

[17] For an overview of the PIMS studies and their impact on strategy, see Buzzell, R. D., and Gale, B. T. (1987), *The PIMS Principles: Linking Strategy to Performance*, New York, Free Press

[18] ibid.

[19] 'Gentlemen, gun your engines', *Business Week*, 10 March, 1997

[20] For a detailed insight into the concept of industry recipes, see Spender, J. C. (1989), *Industry Recipes: The Nature and Sources of Managerial Judgement*, Oxford, Basil Blackwell

[21] ibid.

[22] Bowman, C., and Faulkner, D. (1997), *Competitive and Corporate Strategy*, London, Irwin

23 Parasuraman, A., Zeithaml, V. A., and Berry, L. L. (1985), 'A Conceptual Model of Services Quality and its Implications for Future Research, *Journal of Marketing*, 49, Autumn, 41–50

24 See, for example, Keon, J. W. (1983), 'Product Positioning: Trinodal Mappings of Brand Images and Consumer Preference', *Journal of Marketing Research*, 20 November, 380–92

CHAPTER

2

WHAT IS
STRATEGIC
THINKING?

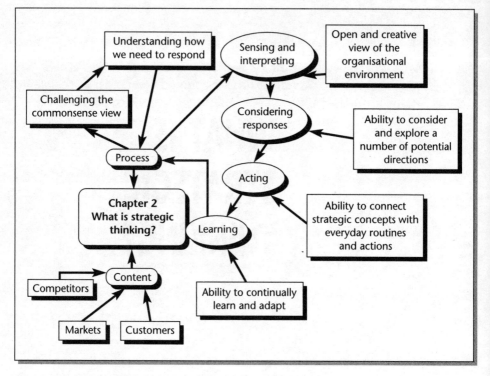

Figure 2.1 Overview map of the subjects covered in Chapter 2

This book is concerned with incorporating customers into strategic thinking. There is an implicit assumption that thinking strategically must be a good thing, but what is it and *is* it a good thing?

As part of the groundwork for Part 2, we need to have a clear sense of what the process of strategic thinking should be in order to be able to apply it in the rest of this book. In this chapter we consider how strategic thinking can be defined and how it occurs in organisations.

Figure 2.1 summarises the core concepts and key elements of this chapter. The core concepts are that strategic thinking can be viewed in terms of content and process. As can be seen, the focus of this chapter is to develop the understanding of strategic thinking as a process. The four element model of the strategic thinking process is shown by means of the ovals. This is explained and explored as a basis for applying strategic thinking to organisations.

HOW CAN WE DEFINE STRATEGIC THINKING?

'Strategic thinking' is a widely used term which has been applied in many differing contexts. One interpretation of the term is that it is concerned with applying frameworks which are designed to give managers insight into the organisational context.

From this perspective, strategic thinking is akin to the planning process. The frameworks applied are therefore largely concerned with understanding the environment in which the organisation operates. These types of framework would typically include Porter's 'five force' model of industry dynamics[1] the ubiquitous SWOT analysis[2] and other planning tools, such as the 'directional policy matrix'[3] and the Boston Consulting Group portfolio matrix.[4] In a lecture to the Strategic Management Society,[5] Lawrence Bossidy of General Electric defined strategic thinking as understanding customers, market conditions and competitors, all of which, he noted, are constantly changing. This perspective is therefore largely concerned with the *content* of strategic thinking. Here the level of analysis is the organisation and the outcome is an understanding of the context in which the organisation finds itself. Here strategic thinking is differentiated from other forms of thinking by a focus on the longer term (although in reality 'long term' is becoming shorter and shorter due to rapid change) and a focus on the issues which impact the whole organisation rather than one particular function or activity. This, therefore, is the subject matter of strategic thinking.

In his book on the mind of the strategist, Kenichi Ohmae refers to the art of strategic thinking.[6] Here he describes the process of disentangling a situation into its component parts:

● ● ●

Faced with problems, trends, events, or situations that appear to constitute a harmonious whole or come packaged as a whole by the common sense of the day, the strategic thinker dissects them into their constituent parts. Then, having discovered the significance of these constituents, he reassembles them in a way calculated to maximise his advantage.

● ● ●

While Ohmae's definition refers to the content of strategic thinking, in terms of the elements and relationships which the business is facing, his perspective differs from the more accepted view in a number of ways. First, he refers to dissecting the elements which may appear to be packaged as a whole. In other words, strategic thinking is not about applying the 'common sense of the day' but is concerned with challenging and understanding this common sense in different ways. In the last sentence, he goes on to emphasise that strategic thinking is also about synthesis – bringing together the elements of analysis and linking these to the potential responses of the organisation. This implies that strategic thinking is a distinctive process as well as a particular level of subject matter. Bossidy's description is concerned with *what* managers are thinking about – customers, markets and competitors. In contrast, Ohmae emphasises *how* managers are thinking – the way in which they appraise a situation and choose to respond to it.

Both of these aspects are important. With regard to content, we are concerned with factors which are external to the organisation. The thought behind this book is that managers should spend more time thinking strategically about their customers because this will generate more clarity and understanding as to how organisations can become more effective. However, it is equally important to reflect on the thinking process and how this may enhance or subvert the development of organisations. The content of strategic thinking is dealt with in subsequent chapters where we consider the role of customers in the strategy of organisations. For the remainder of this chapter we shall consider further the process of strategic thinking and the implications for practice.

In order to consider the process of strategic thinking, we will start by exploring a model of the strategic thinking process. This is outlined in Figure 2.2, which is based on the way in which individuals process information.

Figure 2.2 illustrates the key components of the strategic thinking process. This model is derived from a view of individual information processing. It should be stressed that the model is concerned with strategic thinking at the level of the individual, not of an organisation.

In part 1 of the model, stimuli are sensed and interpreted. This is a vital process as we are bombarded with millions of stimuli every day and, in order to stand any chance of understanding our environment, we need a mechanism which allows us to reduce these stimuli to a manageable number. We filter through only those stimuli which are interpreted as being important. The definition of what is important will be driven by our attentive state. For example, whether we are focused on increasing market share or improving cash flow will affect the types of stimuli we respond to. If we are measured by the corporate centre on our ability to achieve specific market share

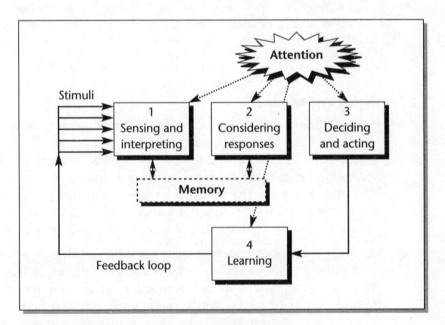

Figure 2.2 A model of the strategic thinking process

targets, say, then a great deal of our resources will be used to pick up stimuli which suggest the activity of competitors and the opportunity to poach some of the larger customers in the industry. However, once we are on course towards achieving these market share objectives, we may focus on actually being able to meet the commitments efficiently in order that our targets for reducing variable costs are achieved.

In addition to our attention levels, sensing and interpreting is also influenced by memory. Our previous experiences, which we hold in our memories, allow us to isolate the particular stimuli which suggest the likelihood of our increasing our market share (such as seeing that a competitor is in trouble, or identifying a group of dissatisfied customers). These will be stimuli which are specific to our own personal experience.

Part 2 of the model represents the process of evaluating the different potential responses which can be made.

In part 3 of the model, we are deciding on particular courses of action and undertaking these actions.

Part 4 represents the phenomenon that once we have acted, we attend to stimuli which give us feedback on these actions. This, in effect, is learning – we are seeking information which gives us feedback as to whether or not our decisions and actions have been the most appropriate ones. Such feedback will then be incorporated into our memories, to be used to pick up on new stimuli and help us assess and suggest particular courses of action.

Each of these component parts is now discussed in further detail.

1 Interpreting and sensing

Strategic thinking is about sensing and interpreting those stimuli which will have wide-ranging and long-term implications for the organisation. In other words, those which have strategic implications for the business. To use Lawrence Bossidy's definition of strategic thinking, this means that we are sensing and interpreting information about customers, competitors and markets, but, importantly, this data is highly dynamic, ambiguous and requires constant reinterpretation.

Research into the way in which managers interpret their environments indicates that previous experience (represented in Figure 2.2 by the 'Memory' box) is strongly influential in terms of interpreting the strategic implications of environmental factors. For example, a study in the USA[7] found that managers interpret new strategic issues as being modified forms of old issues, and, therefore, their responses to them are the same as they were for the old ones. This is most often the case where a previous response had a successful outcome. The new issue may have a number of quite distinctive characteristics, but these are ignored or downplayed because they deviate from the initial interpretation. Let us take as an example a competitor making aggressive inroads into a major distributor. If in the past this has been a short-term initiative in order to boost the company's order levels before its year end, then this is likely to be the way it is interpreted again. However, if the competitor has now changed its strategy and is attempting to sustain its position with the distributor, then this interpretation is no longer appropriate. In fact, it is highly dangerous because it suggests a response which is wholly inappropriate.

One recent example of this has been the retailing of petrol in the UK. Traditionally this has been the domain of the oil majors, with players like BP, Esso and Mobil dominating the market share. For some time, food retailers have been selling petrol at out-of-town sites. The oil majors' rationale was that this was simply a loss-leader to help supermarkets sell groceries and they would never become a significant part of the market. This logic was maintained until the late 1980s and early 1990s, until the multiple retailers began to make major inroads into the oil majors' market share (for some time the oil majors did not even include the retailers in their market share calculations). Now the retailers are major players in the business, with a combined share close to 20 per cent of the market. They have used their retailing expertise to develop the forecourts into convenience stores and are developing the concept of independent petrol outlets, not located on a superstore site.

Another related example is the development of own-label or retailer brands across Europe. Initially this development was interpreted by the food manufacturers as a loss-leader tactic and not a serious long-term threat. Due to information constraints and this attitude, own-label brands were frequently omitted from market share analyses, which assumed that, somehow, own-label products were not competing in the same market as premium brands. In the 1990s, the development of own-label products has burgeoned, with retailers such as Tesco now introducing multiple own-label brands, such as Healthy Eating and Value lines. However, the tendency for the major brands to consider market share without taking own-label products into account persists. Who, then, is thinking strategically here?

There is also evidence that managers are more likely to interpret external stimuli as threats than opportunities,[8] thereby creating a defensive rather than an opportunistic response. A change in technology or buying patterns may have positive and negative interpretations, and while it is important to identify the negative implications of changes in the environment, the positive interpretation may actually hold a number of powerful opportunities. For example, Japanese competition in the off-road vehicle sector was seen as the primary threat by Land Rover in the 1980s and 1990s. However, this 'threat' has also served to generate huge growth in this sector, making four-wheel drive vehicles widely acceptable as, and totally substitutable for, traditional family cars. One interpretation of this for Land Rover would have been that, rather than focusing wholly on beating the Japanese off-road vehicles in a head-on battle, they should position themselves to take advantage of a growing segment with a new profile of customer. In reality this was the outcome, but Land Rover's original intended strategy was indeed focused on beating the Japanese. What emerged, nevertheless, was a generic growth in the four wheel drive sector.[9]

In the sensing and interpreting process, we are reducing a vast amount of external stimuli into smaller sets of information to enable us to understand what is going on. In a strategic situation this is even more significant. Because strategic situations tend to be complicated (involving many interacting variables), ambiguous (the relationships between the variables are very difficult to isolate and determine direction) and uncertain (these variables and their relationships are constantly changing), the process by which we pick and choose from these stimuli in order to form a complete picture has far-reaching implications for the conclusions we will draw and the potential responses we make. Indeed, the Gestalt school of psychology[10] maintains that we sense and interpret based on an emergent whole rather than adding up the smaller stimuli, or *gestalten*. In other words, our sensing and interpretation are not driven by the stimuli themselves, but by our own mindset and the way in which we create a holistic picture of events and circumstances in order to make sense of our environment. An important part of the Gestalt view is that we 'fill in the gaps' of the stimuli in order to create this holistic picture. The way we fill in is shaped by our own experience and judgement. Therefore, the distinction between objective external factors and individual subjectivity becomes increasingly blurred. This is particularly true of phenomena such as stereotyping, where we use certain stimuli to infer things about others which are not immediately obvious. For example, a study in the US army found that officers who were liked by their superiors were judged to be more intelligent than those who were disliked, even though they achieved the same scores in intelligence tests.[11]

The phenomenon of the mindset (I will use this term to refer to the creation of a holistic mental picture, but the terms gestalt, paradigm cognitive map or mental model could also be used) can be observed in the strategic thinking process. In considering the way in which managers identify competition, it has been found that they perceive the number of potential competitors to be fairly small and that they believe them to be similar to themselves. Termed 'cognitive oligopolies',[12] such groupings involve managers seeing themselves in a far smaller and more controllable competitive situation than might be concluded by an outside observer. This also means that they are able to infer the nature of the competitive responses they might expect, whereas organisations about which they have very little knowledge or understanding, which they would have trouble making predictions about, do not figure in their mindset about what constitutes the competition. There are many examples of where a commonly held mindset of the industry has masked the threat of new entrants – Virgin moving into financial services, direct banking and insurance, and food retailers moving into selling fuel to name but a few. Later in the book we shall see how the mindset we hold of our customers can also be highly simplistic and potentially restrict our ability to build competitive advantage.

There is a natural tendency for us to simplify the complexity of the environment in order to enable us to interpret it effectively. This simplification is based on past cues and experiences which we use to create a coherent picture or mindset based on our own experiences. The advantage of 'experience', therefore, is that it gives us a wide range of differing models to draw on in order to understand a situation and the appropriate response to it. However, the richness of experience is not based simply on time. A question which often goes unasked is whether or not the individual who claims to have 20 years' experience really does or whether they just have a year's experience which happens to be 20 years old. Experience is also about the ability reflect and learn from events rather than to simply put up the same list of prescriptive answers every time a problem is faced. Experience in the context of strategic thinking is therefore concerned with the flexibility and adaptability of our mindsets.

In summary, the basis of strategic sensing and interpreting is that we are able to identify those stimuli which are strategically significant to the business and to challenge and reevaluate these stimuli in order to avoid making a simplistic interpretation based on past behaviours. The antithesis of strategic sensing and interpretation is a narrow view of the external environment which only picks up stimuli which are easily identifiable from past experiences and events. One such example is given in Levitt's seminal paper 'Marketing Myopia'.[13] Levitt relates the problems of businesses such as railroad companies, which failed to identify threats from road and air because they defined their market as railroads rather than transportation. In other words, their sensing and interpretation was driven by a product view of the environment and, therefore, they looked for stimuli which related to the product area rather than stimuli which impacted on the wider provision of meeting customers' needs.

The implication of this discussion is that for strategic thinking to occur, mechanisms are needed to avoid the natural inclination to reduce the environment to an oversimplified mindset which masks substantial threats ('But they're not really competitors are they?') and/or opportunities ('We're in a declining, highly competitive market so there's very little we can do'). One potential approach is to use techniques such as scenario development as a way of acknowledging the possibility of multiple interpretations of the environment and, therefore, being sensitive to the stimuli which may suggest these differing possibilities. The rationale for scenario approaches is that organisations are dealing with increasingly unpredictable environments which require more sensitivity to quite radical changes in direction. These radical changes are not identified in traditional approaches to interpretation, which are largely based on trend extrapolation (an elaborate way of saying that the future is predicted on the basis of what has happened in the past).

Van der Heijden[14] refers to scenario planning as a way of enhancing corporate perception. He uses the example of Royal Dutch Shell in the oil crisis of 1973. Shell has been largely seen as the originator and developer of scenario planning approaches in organisations. Indeed, many of the seminal works on scenario planning have been written by corporate planners who were with Shell.[15] Prior to 1973, the situation in the oil industry had been one of rapid increases in demand, with supply and the availability of refining capacity being the key restraint on organisational growth. In this context, the mindset of the oil majors was that they should be concerned with increasing capacity in order to build shares by meeting demand. Shell had developed a number of alternative scenarios, one of which was that, in time, the governments of the producing countries may not continue to supply the levels of oil needed by the oil companies. When this crisis actually began to materialise in 1973, Shell was able to identify the signals which were consistent with this scenario. Shell was therefore able to interpret and respond to these stimuli in a way which was far more effective than were the actions of their competitors. For many, this was the point at which Shell shifted from being a middle-ranking oil company to becoming one of the major world players.[16]

Figure 2.3 summarises the potential of scenarios for opening out conventional mindsets. Here we see the conventional interpretation of stimuli, which is based on a myopic or bounded mindset. This mindset expects particular types of stimuli to suggest future actions. The scenario approach, however, opens up new possibilities as to which stimuli may be important in the future.

2 Considering responses

As with sensing and interpreting, our experience, captured in memory, is influential in determining which responses have worked in the past and, therefore, which of them should work again. The danger is that we do not seriously consider any alternative responses because our interpretation of the stimuli has channelled us into a preselected response. In order to simplify the information-processing activity, we will inevitably try to achieve shortcuts by associating the present with previous situations in order to draw up some options.

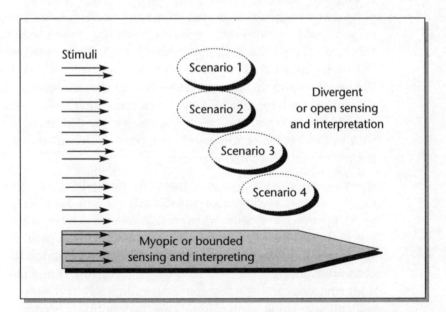

Figure 2.3 Contrasting myopic and divergent sensing and interpretation

Within many industries, there are various 'recipes' for what the usual options and responses are. The response to a price war, the response to a new entrant have all happened before and are perpetuated by our need to simplify and formulate responses based on our own experience. In industrial situations, organisations which were able to sell themselves out of trouble by running aggressive sales campaigns, filling up the distribution channel, suddenly find that these responses no longer work. The basis on which they were successful (reactive distributors with relatively slack control systems) no longer apply. They are then responding to a situation in the usual way, they are not thinking strategically. They are, in effect, responding to yesterday's stimuli, not tomorrow's. However, it is often difficult to identify whether or not it is the mindset which is restricting our choice of responses. After all, we are all relatively sophisticated in dressing up our logic in way which does not create the impression that we are simply going to respond in the same way we did last time. We may use some new terms, such as customer-focused teams, or systematically exceeding customer expectations, but, actually, it is the same old response wearing some new clothes.

One example of this is the infamous Sinclair C5.[17] Sir Clive Sinclair developed an electric vehicle which he claimed was targeted at the second car market, to be used by a spouse in everyday activities such as shopping, or, alternatively, replacing the noisy mopeds which pubescent teenagers ride around on making as much ear-splitting noise as possible. However, it was clear, certainly in hindsight, that these were not serious customer groups, but a latter rationalisation as to who might possibly buy the C5. The strategy had not been built on the notion of entering the market for second cars, the strategy had already been determined: Sir Clive had a vision that electric vehicles were the way forward and everything else was post-rationalised to fit with this vision. The sensing and interpretation were used to support the predetermined course of action.

It is also important to recognise that considering different responses has the effect of forcing us to consider other external stimuli and to be sensitive to other issues which would have been ignored had we just proceeded down one single, only-rationalised-later path. For example, for an organisation in the synthetic fibres business to consider divesting itself of its manufacturing capability and building up the research and development activity in which it is already recognised as being particularly strong, may not have been the obvious response to an extremely competitive fibres market where it is increasingly difficult to grow the business. The conventional wisdom would probably have been that the firm should find the niche markets which are growing, or at least not declining as fast, and focus on these while managing costs and scaling down operations. However, in seriously considering this option, the management team found that there are more opportunities to develop their expertise and market it through the sale of particular licences and products. These opportunities would not have been uncovered if the organisation had perpetuated its original mindset of growing the business by launching and manufacturing heavily patented fibres.

The strategic approach to considering responses is that a number of diverse responses are considered. These will generate further understanding of the environmental dynamics and the internal capabilities of the organisation and will enable a more measured decision to be made. The antithesis of this perspective is that the response is preselected and the sensing and interpretation of the environment is used to rationalise a particular selection after the event.

3 Deciding and acting

One aspect of the model in Figure 2.2, in common with many other strategy process models, is that it implies that actions come after thinking, that there is a clear distinction between the stages, each being discrete and separate and requiring different approaches. This is not the impression which this model is intended to give. The purpose of the model is to clarify and explain the process, but if it implies that action is some discrete disconnected stage then it is not concerned with strategic thinking. The position of this text is similar to that taken by Karl Weick,[18] which is that actions are not an outcome of thinking or sensemaking but are interactively linked, that thinking defines action and actions define thinking:

● ● ●

The beliefs make sense of the irrevocable action and the circumstance in which it was generated, even if all of this was only vaguely clear when the action became irrevocable. It is the committed act in search of an explanation that anchors this form of sensemaking.

Weick[18]

● ● ●

43

For this reason, acting or behaviour is a central part, rather than an outcome, of the strategic thinking process. While we are dealing with it as one of the four elements, each of these four is inseparable from the whole process. We have already considered some of the pathologies of strategic thinking – namely myopia or tunnel vision – both in terms of sensing and interpreting the environment and in terms of considering multiple responses to the external stimuli. However, there is one more distinctive pathology, which is when strategic thinking is viewed as a wholly cerebral, conceptual process, untainted by the rudeness of action or the true test of implementation. These issues are considered in some depth in Chapter 7, but the inseparability of strategic thinking from action is worthy of further exploration here.

One of the problems with the term 'strategic thinking' is that it appears to discount action or behaviour as part of its agenda. The pathology of the intellectual strategy is one which involves sophisticated sensing and multiple interpretations and the complicated assessment of options. However, a clear course of action remains unclear or certainly unachievable. Indeed, the actual actions which need to be undertaken seem almost secondary to the process of intellectualising and drafting the strategy.

Much of the academic work on strategy processes has tended to focus on the stages of sensing and interpreting and the consideration of multiple responses or strategic options. There are those who believe that this work is missing the point of what really happens in organisations. In fact, too much analysis can be dysfunctional and create a kind of analysis paralysis which inhibits rather than enhances strategic thinking. This is summarised in Figure 2.4.

A long-time critic of the rational planning school of strategy, Henry Mintzberg[19] refers to the planning dilemma, which is that the weight of techniques and systems needed to analyse the strategic situations of large companies have turned them into lumbering bureaucracies numbed by their planning systems. He roundly criticises the traditional planning school for being restricted by a rational, linear approach to strategy where implementation is what happens at the end, almost as an after-thought, rather than being the axis for the whole process.

In support of this view, there is evidence to suggest that those who are able to make the links between actions and interpretation are able to produce a more effective organisational response than those who can

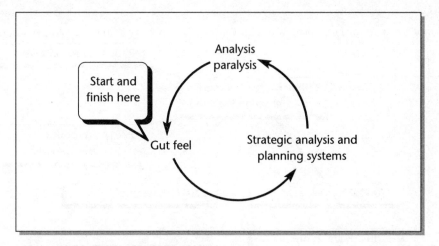

Figure 2.4 The analysis paralysis loop

do all the analysis, but are still unsure as to what actions to follow. For example, in a study of the owner-managers of independent retail businesses,[20] all those interviewed demonstrated a common understanding of who the customer was, what they wanted and the nature of competition and, to return to the discussion at the start of the chapter, these individuals could think strategically using Lawrence Bossidy's definition – that is, they were thinking about customers, competitors and markets. However, in comparing levels of performance of those who were growing rapidly and those who were static or declining, those who were growing, according to a series of measures, were those who connected their understanding of the environment to the capabilities of the business. The output of their thinking was not just an understanding of their situation, but an understanding of what they could and should do to respond to it. This is illustrated in Figure 2.5.

Here the owner-manager shows a clear understanding of why a refit is necessary in her small pharmacy business. It is this ability to link actions with a complicated analysis of the environment which is the real strategic challenge, not the need for ever more sophisticated environmental analysis.

In a study of organisational change in two US railroad companies,[21] it was found that both companies recognised the threats of deregulation and how it might change their business, both were good at analytical thinking, but only one was able to understand how its own

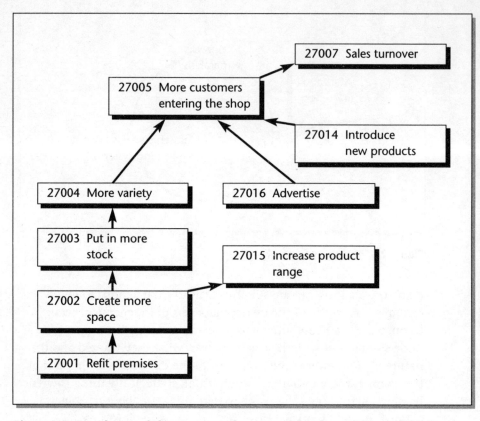

Figure 2.5 Causal map of the manager of a successful independent retail business
Source: Jenkins and Johnson[20]

capabilities would help it to respond to these environmental changes, and this was the organisation which ultimately survived these changes. It is the synthesis of external and internal analysis into clear actions and the redefining of analysis following actions which defines the process of strategic thinking.

The issue which sets actions apart from the stages of sensing, interpretation and considering responses is that it requires the convergent thinking and single-mindedness which is also deemed to create the marketing myopia to which Levitt refers. However, in this case, myopia is an asset rather than a liability. It is a natural response to the complexity of the world. In order to function effectively as human beings and as managers, we need to have the ability to reduce the complexity of our surroundings. Otherwise, we would simply go mad trying to process every single stimuli to which we are exposed.

There are various studies which indicate that strategies which are simple, coherent and easily understood may lead to better performance than those which are sophisticated and highly complicated.[22] Tunnel vision can also help meld an organisation together to deliver a particular strategy. The Naskapi Indians in North America burn caribou bones and their priests read the cracks in the bones to predict where the best hunting is to be found.[23] This is pure myopia, but the hunters do not spend their time arguing, they get on and hunt and invariably find the game they anticipate.

In a review of company mission statements, Grant[24] notes the contrast between mission statements which follow Levitt's divergent view and those which are deliberately myopic in order to introduce clarity and focus to the organisation. For example, Merrill Lynch and others describe their mission as 'to serve the full range of financial needs to our customers'. This is in stark contrast to that of the 3M Corporation, which is concerned with 'the application of adhesive and thin-film technology to new product development'. Neither approach is necessarily right or wrong. The important issue for strategic thinking is that we need both myopic and divergent ways of seeing things. The challenge is being able to move between the two and to know which to use and when.

4 Learning

The terms strategic thinking and strategic learning are often used interchangeably. In this context we are considering learning as a feedback loop which allows us to sense and interpret new or modified stimuli, providing us with an indication of the results of our actions. However, of course, this learning loop is subject to all the problems of myopic thinking discussed above. We are more likely to be attuned to the stimuli which bring evidence of the correctness of our actions and to discount or ignore those which suggest that our course of action was not the best one, for example.

Important concepts to consider regarding learning are single- and double-loop learning.[25] Single-loop learning is that which takes place within the established assumptions or mindset of the individual. For example, if market share figures are falling, then a promotional campaign is introduced to help recover share. The feedback from the results of the campaign is then interpreted and a form of learning takes place regarding the effectiveness or otherwise of the promotional campaign. In this case, the variables (market share, promotional campaign expenditure) are clearly defined. The learning therefore occurs within this particular context.

Double-loop learning, on the other hand, involves a revision of the variables themselves and their interrelationships. For example, the same organisation decides to create further growth by increasing customer retention, while also building market share, basing this strategy on the development of a customer service operation, and it is very successful. However, as it develops, it begins to identify that customer retention levels are being constrained by how the salesforce develops relationships with customers, which in turn is linked to the way that salespeople's work is currently measured and rewarded. This is double-loop learning because the new initiative has raised a whole set of issues which challenge the basis on which the business has been operating. The challenge of double-loop learning, therefore, is whether or not individuals are able to loosen up their current mindset in order to be able to challenge and revisit some of the basic assumptions regarding the way in which their organisation and environment operate.

The feedback, or learning, loop shown in Figure 2.2 is concerned with how we sense and interpret our own actions. It almost implies that we are somehow objectively able to evaluate our own responses. However, research which has been undertaken on a range of organisations finds that managers show consistent patterns in the way they explain the reasons for the performance of the business.[26] To summarise, when businesses are successful, performance is attributed to the ability of the management team, but when businesses are unsuccessful, performance is attributed to the hostility of the environment, in particular 'unfair' or 'irrational' competition or 'unnecessary' or 'short-sighted' government regulations. This is a perfectly natural response in most organisations. Someone who stands up and says 'I got it wrong' or 'We've been successful because we've been lucky' is unlikely to enjoy the adulation of their peers and even less likely to make a rapid progression to the upper echelons of the organisation. However, it is these very behaviours that may be the way to enhance our capability to think strategically because otherwise we are not learning from what goes wrong or what goes right. Success which goes unquestioned is success which is not understood and therefore cannot be managed and therefore replicated. In particular, it seems that it is more likely that the nature of success will go unchallenged than with failure, with potentially disastrous results.

This ability to continually take and learn from feedback is at the heart of strategic thinking. This works for both success and failure. For example, a large brewery which was created as a result of the merger of two medium-sized businesses had lost 7 per cent of its on-trade market share customers (on-trade is the term used for the sale of beer to licensed premises for consumption on the premises) because of the way in which these had been handled post-merger (there had been a good number of missed deliveries during this period). This experience has never been forgotten and a recent reorganisation, to improve the efficiency of the business, was undertaken with the specific criteria that customer disturbance was to be kept to a minimum. This imposed unrealistic constraints on the new operations, which were restricted as to how far they could change their sales areas. While most of the profitable customers had tenants who changed frequently and who, therefore, could not remember the 'bad old days', the company insisted on a set of restrictions that undermined all the benefits which were expected to come from the reorganisation. In this case, the organisation was still in single-loop learning – it did not reassess the assumptions on which these restrictions had been based.

In their review of the reasons for the Challenger space shuttle disaster, Starbuck and Milliken[27] concluded that the past success of the shuttle had led NASA to be less critical of its own abilities to identify and resolve potentially catastrophic problems. In 1985, NASA had requested that old problems be closed out (that is, no longer listed as a launch constraint). The 'O' ring problem which caused the disaster was deemed to be one such old problem.

Past success increases confidence in the way things are done which makes it far more difficult to challenge and change them, the implication being that success stultifies strategic thinking. Ironically, therefore, failure may be more valuable than success in terms of developing strategic thinking. Thus, the notion of exploring the root causes of customer defection is promoted by many of those who believe that customer retention strategies are central to organisational success. There may be more opportunity to analyse what has happened and to improve the organisational response to customers by dissecting failure where the elements can be more easily determined than by assessing success where the customer may be less able to articulate the reasons for the ongoing relationship.

What can we conclude from our model?

The conclusion that we can infer from our discussion is that these elements need to be in balance. If actions take over sensing, then the learning will be an impoverished process. Similarly, if sensing and considering different responses take precedence over action, then nothing happens. Strategic thinking is therefore as much about the linkage between these elements as it is about the elements themselves. It is not simply a case of being able to consider multiple interpretations or multiple options, it is about connecting these multiple possibilities with some clear actions and understanding the implications of this process. One of the ways in which scenario planning is used is as a basis for testing out a strategy which has already been implemented, to identify where the vulnerabilities may be. Here, sensing and interpretation follow on from actions. We have some way to go in understanding the nature and true impact of strategic thinking, but we are in a position to make some informed judgements about how this process works and how it may work better.

So, does it work? If we become strategic thinkers does this guarantee success? The honest answer has to be 'No'. However, the research which has been presented in this chapter, does indicate that individuals and organisations who are able to integrate analysis with

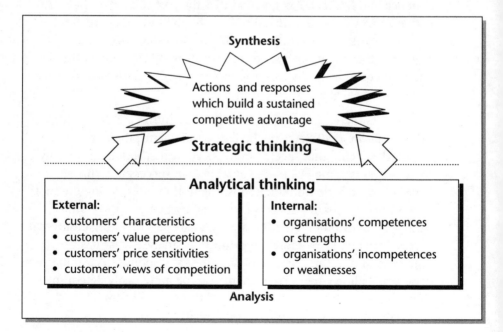

Synthesis

Actions and responses which build a sustained competitive advantage

Strategic thinking

Analytical thinking

External:
- customers' characteristics
- customers' value perceptions
- customers' price sensitivities
- customers' views of competition

Internal:
- organisations' competences or strengths
- organisations' incompetences or weaknesses

Analysis

Figure 2.6 The nature of strategic thinking

synthesis are more effective in distilling, communicating and implementing strategies. Above all, it provides a basis for understanding, and therefore feeling equal to, the environment in which we are operating. Comfort can be soporific and anxiety can make us even more dysfunctional, but, for many organisations, anxiety rules over comfort. If nothing else, the notion of strategic thinking provides a basis for questioning, stimulating and energising the organisation. An organisation which thrives on strategic thinking is likely to be an exciting and stimulating place to be in.

The notion of strategic thinking applied in this book is that of analysis: understanding customers and understanding the organisation, which has to be followed by synthesis. Synthesis is the key step which differentiates strategic thinking from analytical thinking (see Figure 2.6). Synthesis is concerned with interpreting and connecting the external analysis with the internal understanding of the organisation and, therefore, developing a clear basis on which to act. It is about developing clear actions and priorities from the analysis.

KEY SUMMARY POINTS

1 Strategic thinking is specific in its content or area of concern (such as customers, competitors, markets), but is a distinct process which also deals with complicated, ambiguous and uncertain data sources.

2 Strategic thinking is an iterative process which links sensing, interpreting, considering responses, acting and learning.

3 The effect of a mindset is that we tend to restrict our interpretation of new information to situations which we have experienced in the past.

4 The effect of a mindset often is that we have a predetermined solution and collect the environmental data to support this.

5 Divergent techniques, such as scenario development, can assist in making us think outside the existing mindset.

6 Acting and thinking are interconnected: we act to help us understand a situation and we understand situations in order to act.

7 Learning can either be within the existing mindset (single-loop learning) or can involve stretching the mindset by challenging and changing its underlying assumptions (double-loop learning).

KEY QUESTIONS AND DIAGNOSTICS

Can you identify a mindset which affects the way you interpret new data, consider potential responses, take a particular course of action and learn from this?

Think of a recent significant event in the organisational environment. What was the response? How many other responses could have been made?

Ignoring the external world temporarily, write down the three most important actions you think the organisation should undertake. What are the external events which would make these actions very successful? Which external events would make these actions disastrous for the organisation. What does this tell you?

STRATEGIC THINKING DIAGNOSTIC

Score each of these statements in terms of how strongly you agree or disagree with them. Add up the scores and see what your total means.

	Agree			Disagree	
	1	2	3	4	5
In our organisation, strategy is a ritual that has little bearing on what we do from day to day.	1	2	3	4	5
We know exactly what is going to happen in our industry.	1	2	3	4	5
There is really only one way to respond to the environment.	1	2	3	4	5
We rarely make changes to the way we do things.	1	2	3	4	5
We frequently reappraise a whole load of assumptions which we have made about the way we do things.	1	2	3	4	5
We rarely change our strategy – once it is in the plan, that is it for the next five years.	1	2	3	4	5
Strategy is something that we do in the first two weeks of August, then we get back to our real jobs.	1	2	3	4	5

Score

25–35: Strategic thinking is alive and well.

15–25: There is evidence of life, but not as we'd like it, Jim.

0–15: Strategically brain-dead: seek resuscitation or find a new job.

SUGGESTED FURTHER READING

There are a number of books around on strategic thinking. Some of the following are worth considering.

Argyris, C., and Schon, D.A. (1978), *Organizational Learning: A Theory of Action Perspective*, Reading, MA, Addison-Wesley

Huff, A. S. (1990), *Mapping Strategic Thought*, Chichester, John Wiley

Ohmae, K. (1982), *The Mind of the Strategist*, New York, McGraw-Hill

Weick, K. E. (1995), *Sensemaking in Organisations*, Thousand Oaks, CA, Sage

REFERENCES

[1] Porter, M. (1980), *Competitive Strategy*, New York, Free Press

[2] Learned, E., Christiansen, C., Andrews, K., and Guth, W. (1969), *Business Policy*, Homewood, Il, Irwin

[3] Robinson, S. J. Q., Hitchens, R. E., and Wade, D. P. (1978), 'The Directional Policy Matrix – Tool for Strategic Planning', *Long Range Planning*, June, 8–15

[4] For a review of this approach, see Day, G. S. (1977), 'Diagnosing the Product Portfolio', *Journal of Marketing*, April, 29–38

[5] Bossidy, L. A. (1987), 'Some thoughts on Strategic Thinking', copy of presentation to the Strategic Management Society, Boston, MA

[6] Ohmae, K. (1982), *The Mind of the Strategist*, New York, McGraw-Hill

[7] Dutton, J. E. (1993), 'Interpretations on Automatic: A Different View of Strategic Issue Diagnosis', *Journal of Management Studies*, 30, 3, 339–57

[8] Dutton, J. E., Walton, E. J., and Abrahamson, E. (1989), 'Important Dimensions of Strategic Issues: Separating the Wheat from the Chaff', *Journal of Management Studies*, 26, 4, July, 379–96

[9] Peck, H. (1992), 'Land Rover Discovery – A Case Study', European Case Clearing House, Cranfield School of Management

[10] Koffka, K. (1935), *Principles of Gestalt Psychology*, New York, Harcourt Brace, and Kohler, W. (1947), *Gestalt Psychology: An Introduction to New Concepts in Modern Psychology*, New York, Liveright

[11] Grove, B. A., and Kerr, W. A. (1951), 'Specific Evidence on Origin of Halo Effect in Measurement of Morale', *Journal of Social Psychology*, 34, 165–70

[12] Porac, J. F., and Thomas, H. (1990), 'Taxonomic Mental Models in Competitor Definition', *Academy of Management Review*, 15, 2, 224–40

[13] Levitt, T. (1960), 'Marketing Myopia, *Harvard Business Review*, July–August, 45–56

[14] Van der Heijden, K. (1996), *Scenarios: The Art of Strategic Conversation*, Chichester, John Wiley

15 For example, Wack, P. (1985), 'Scenarios: Shooting the Rapids', *Harvard Business Review*, November–December, 139–50, and Schwartz, P. (1991), *The Art of the Long View*, New York, Doubleday

16 Mack, T. (1989), 'Time, Money and Patience', *Forbes*, August 21, 60–2

17 Marks, A. P. (1986), 'The Sinclair C5 – Why Did it Fail?, *Management Decision*, **28**, 4, 9–14

18 Weick, K. E. (1995), *Sensemaking in Organisations*, Thousand Oaks, CA, Sage

19 Mintzberg, H. (1994), *The Rise and Fall of Strategic Planning*, Hemel Hempstead, Prentice Hall

20 Jenkins, M., and Johnson, G. (1996), 'Linking Managerial Cognition and Organisational Performance: Some Insights From the Retail Sector', paper presented at the British Academy of Management Annual Conference, Aston Business School

21 Barr, P. S., Stimpert, J. L., and Huff, A. S. (1992), 'Cognitive Change, Strategic Action, and Organizational Renewal', *Strategic Management Journal*, **13**, Summer special issue, 15–36

22 Conant, J. S., Mokwa, M. P., and Varadarajan, P. R. (1990), 'Strategic Types, Distinctive Marketing Competencies and Organizational Performance: A Multiple Measures-based Study', *Strategic Management Journal*, **11**, September, 365–83, and Covin, J. G., Slevin, D. P., and Covin, T. J. (1990), 'Content and Performance of Growth-Seeking Strategies: A Comparison of Small Firms in High- and Low-technology Industries', *Journal of Business Venturing*, **5**, 6, November, 391–412

23 Speck, F. G. (1977), *Naskapi*, Norman, University of Oklahoma

24 Grant, R. M. (1991), *Contemporary Strategy Analysis: Concepts, Techniques, Applications*, Cambridge, MA, Blackwells

25 Argyris, C., and Schon D.A. (1978), *Organizational Learning: A Theory of Action Perspective*, Reading, MA, Addison-Wesley

26 For example, 'Salancik, G. R., and Meindl, J. R. (1984), 'Corporate Attributions as Strategic Illusions of Control,' *Administrative Science Quarterly*, **29**, June, 238–54, Huff, A. S., and Schwenk, C. R. (1990), 'Bias and Sensemaking in Good Times and Bad', in Huff, A. S. (Ed.), *Mapping Strategic Thought*, Chichester, John Wiley, 89–108, and Clapham, S. E., and Schwenk, C. R. (1991), Self-serving Attributions, Managerial Cognition, and Company Performance, *Strategic Management Journal*, **12**, 219–29

27 Starbuck, W. H., and Milliken, F. J. (1988), 'Challenger: Fine-tuning the Odds Until Something Breaks', *Journal of Management Studies*, **25**; 319–40

PART 2

THE PROCESS: THINKING STRATEGICALLY ABOUT CUSTOMERS

CHAPTER

3

AN OVERVIEW
OF PART 2

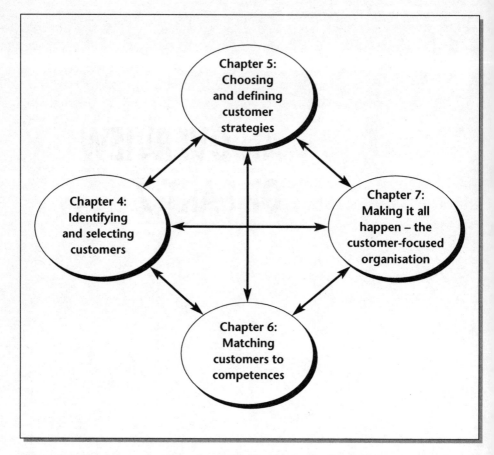

Figure 3.1 The four main elements of thinking strategically about customers covered in Part 2

Part 1 established the arguments for a shift in the way we consider the strategic context of the organisation and the strategic directions which can be taken. These arguments are based on the premise that the accepted wisdom of focusing on markets is no longer the basis on which future advantage can be built. This can only be achieved by means of a detailed understanding of the organisation's links with its customers. In order to develop this understanding, Part 2 is concerned with outlining the four main elements involved in the process of understanding and managing the linkages between customers and an organisation.

THINKING STRATEGICALLY ABOUT CUSTOMERS: THE MENTAL MAP

Figure 3.1 shows the basic structure of the rest of Part 2. There is a chapter about each of the four central elements and each contains a series of questions concerning the application of a customer-based approach to strategy. While the chapters are arranged in a linear way due to the physical constraints of bookbinding, as you can see from Figure 3.1, they are intended to be iterative. Thus, once you have read the chapters through, the elements can be approached from any point and, indeed, constant movement around the elements is required in order to refine the strategy. As we move around the elements, we are revisiting and amending differing assumptions until we have a sense that a coherent strategy has emerged.

Let us now outline the four elements in the order in which they appear.

Chapter 4

In Chapter 4 we start by asking the rudimentary but fundamental question 'Who are our customers?'. Here we are not taking the position of many total quality and customer service proponents who suggest that everyone is the supplier and the customer. In this context, we are concerned with focusing on customers who are external to the organisation (whatever this may mean) as we believe that this gives the necessary clarity to the customer groups which bring all the benefits outlined in Chapter 1.

The question of identifying customer groups is particularly important as it has far-reaching implications, yet it is rarely raised in organisations, it is assumed that there is a common mindset as to who the customers are and how they should be served. In addition to clarifying this issue, Chapter 4 provides a framework for defining those customers who are strategically important to the organisation. This aspect is developed in subsequent chapters – in Chapter 5, with the development of the strategic customer profile, and in Chapter 6 where we consider how particular customers may be linked to the competences of the organisation. The third element, covered in Chapter 4, is the consideration of future changes to the nature and identity of customers. Having spent a large part of Chapter 2 considering the importance of an open approach to sensing and interpretation, we apply a scenario development process to key customer groups in order to consider some of the different issues which can be developed from customer-based scenarios.

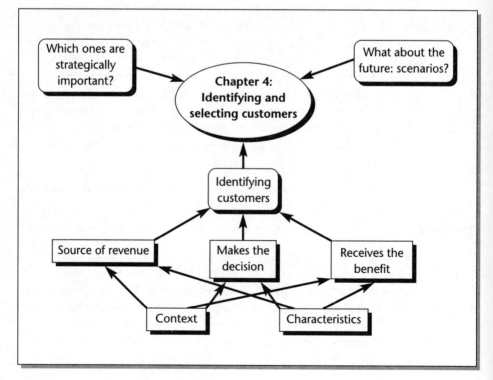

Figure 3.2 Overview map of Chapter 4

The content of Chapter 4 is summarised in Figure 3.2. You can see that this chapter addresses two central questions about customers – who they are now and who they need to be in the future, given the relative importance of different customer groups and the way things may change in the future.

Chapter 5

Having introduced a set of processes for identifying and selecting customers, we now consider potential customer strategies. Although referring back to Chapter 2, the emphasis here is on considering some of the alternative responses which an organisation can make to the customer environment. Chapter 5 considers three elements of customer strategy: direction, focus and positioning.

In order to consider the direction of strategy, we use an adapted form of the stoic Ansoff matrix, termed the customer growth matrix, to consider where the overall organisational orientation should be developed. At all times, we try to avoid a simplistic 'pick the box' approach and have raised the importance of understanding how these different categories can be combined to create a stronger momentum.

In considering the focus of the customer strategy, we relate the discussion back to the issues covered in Chapter 4, in particular, the identification of those customers who are seen to be strategically important to the organisation. By clarifying which customers are central to the development of the organisation, we can create a strategic customer profile to bring clarity and focus to our activities.

Finally, with regard to positioning, we consider Cliff Bowman's customer matrix as a basis for identifying the competitive position in the eyes of the customer and the competitive moves which are open to us. The practical applications of this model are explained and the potential ways in which competitors may position themselves in their customers' perceptions of them.

Figure 3.3 summarises the elements and relationships which make up Chapter 5.

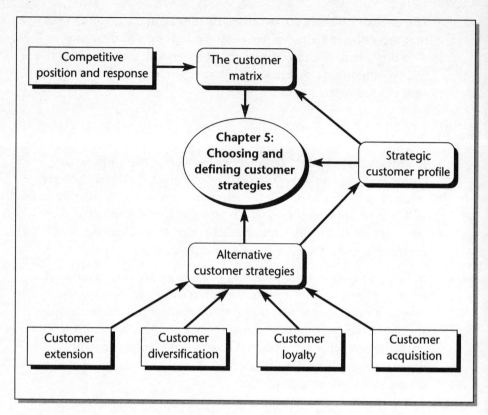

Figure 3.3 Overview map of Chapter 5

Chapter 6

Chapter 6 moves more deeply into an examination and analysis of the internal workings of the organisation and considers the competences of the organisation which allow the development of a sustained competitive advantage. These are therefore competences which are both rare and difficult for competitors to copy or substitute.

The concept of 'competence' is taken a step further by exploring the linkages between competences and the dimensions of value and price used by customers to assess the overall value of the product or service. This emphasises the continued iteration needed between inside-out factors (competences) and outside-in factors (the value assessments made by the customers). It also introduces a further perspective for defining strategic actions, which, in this case, is to develop or add to customer value in a way which matches the competences of the organisation or to build on those competences which are going to add value to customers.

Figure 3.4 summarises the key elements of Chapter 6.

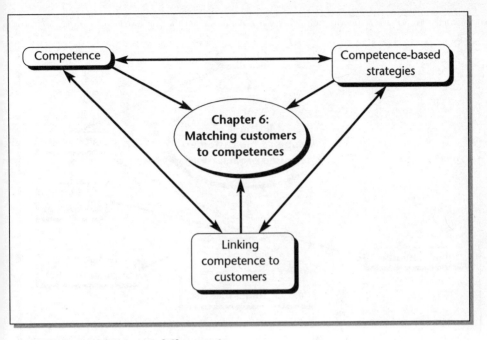

Figure 3.4 Overview map of Chapter 6

Chapter 7

Having considered the conceptual dimensions of the four elements of the customer–organisation relationship, Chapter 7 considers the questions surrounding the actions needed to implement these ideas – in other words, to turn a set of conceptual ideas into a strategy.

In this chapter we explore the power of the organisational mindset in both positive terms, by creating a sustainable competitive advantage, and in negative terms, by resisting the intended strategy designed to enhance the development of the organisation.

A number of elements are used to formulate an effective approach to implementation. These include an assessment of the stereotypical views which those within the organisation have of their customers, and the cultural factors which impact on the relationship between the organisation and those customers which are regarded as the basis of long-term advantage. Here, Gerry Johnson's Culture Web is used to surface some of the dimensions of organisational culture. This chapter concludes by considering some of the approaches to organisational change which may be applied to develop a customer-focused organisation.

Figure 3.5 summarises the key elements involved in building the customer-focused organisation.

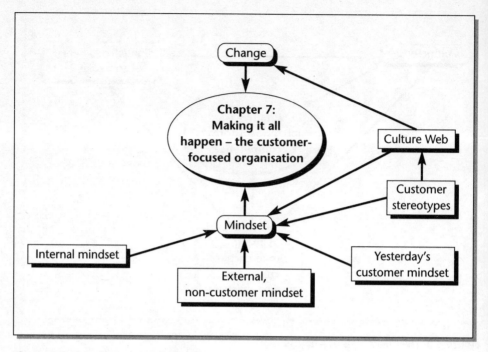

Figure 3.5 Overview map of Chapter 7

Using what you have learned

Analysis tools, such as those presented in the following chapters, do not, of themselves, make strategic decisions. They generate thought, stimulate questions about the environment, about the business and its capabilities. It is not suggested that the elements discussed replace all the frameworks and heuristics which managers are already using to help them in their strategic thinking. Rather, that this presents an alternative to the 'market mindset', introducing the clarity and insight which a 'customer mindset' brings. Like all frameworks, it is not perfect and sometimes requires certain leaps of judgement, but that, thankfully is the basis on which people and their creative abilities will always make the key difference in organisations. However, it is hoped that the questions it raises lead directly back to generating a strategy which is both advantageous and sustainable.

In summary, the four elements of good customer–organisation relationships are, first, a clear definition of who the customers are and therefore the recipients of the strategy and the sources of future returns, one that understands the diversity and complexity of customers and acknowledges differences but also focuses on the key customer groups and their requirements. Second, clarification on the strategies available to the organisation in terms of direction, focus and positioning. Third, knowing the organisation's competences and how these link with customers' needs. Fourth, allowing the organisation to assess and implement the changes needed to build a more coherent customer focus and thereby maximise the relationship with the customer.

However, the process, in reality, is iterative. Therefore the mental maps show the territory which needs to be understood, but do not give a specific route to follow. It is hoped that in the subsequent chapters your assumptions will be challenged, new ideas formed and old ones redeveloped, in a similar vein to the double-loop learning process outlined in Chapter 2. Above all, this framework is about strategic thinking and creativity and if it generates some ideas and challenges some assumptions then it will have achieved its aim.

IDENTIFYING
AND SELECTING
CUSTOMERS

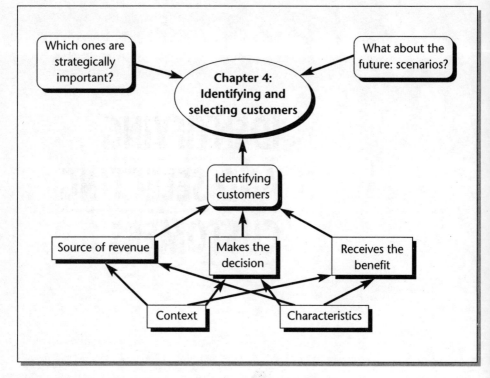

Figure 4.1 An outline of the concepts covered in this chapter

This chapter deals with a series of simple questions about customers. Who are they and which are the customers who will be most advantageous for our organisation, both now and in the future? These questions are summarised by the core concepts outlined in Figure 4.1. This diagram outlines the area which will be covered in this chapter. We start by identifying the customers of the organisation.

STARTING AT THE BEGINNING

Who are our customers? Perhaps a self-evident question in some organisations, but undoubtedly less evident in many more. The term 'customers' is used quite liberally in organisational dialogue, but are we talking about the same individuals or organisations?

At one strategy workshop, a wide debate was taking place on the role of customers in the organisation. The group consisted of general managers of a mixture of nationalities from a global organisation. They were all affably discussing the importance of customers when it became apparent that there were two contrasting views in the room as to who their customers actually were. In this case, the company was involved with logistics, a significant area of its business being groceries. The discussion centred on whether or not the company's customer was the grocery retailer (which effectively dominated the supply chain) or the food manufacturer (which paid for the service).

In this kind of situation, defining who our customers are is not just a matter of semantics, it is central to the strategic focus of the organisation. As one of the managers put it in the above discussion. 'If we don't have the right customer, our eye is off the ball – we're spending our time looking in the wrong direction'. If everyone agrees the customers are important, but then they go away and fervently apply this to totally different groups, the organisation is at best no further forward and at worst in absolute confusion. This may alienate the customers who could help secure long-term advantage for the organisation. So, just how *do* you define your customers?

Customers can be described in two ways. First, on the basis of their characteristics as individuals or organisations. Second, they can be described by the context in which they buy and consume the product or service. For example, among airlines there is now a relatively clear assumption that the market can be readily segmented between business and leisure travel. Business travellers use 'business class' and those visiting friends and relatives (VFR) or on holiday use 'economy class'. One particular person may be both a business and leisure traveller at different times, but, in these two different contexts, they will respond quite differently, both in terms of the way in which they buy and the criteria used. While this person is the same individual in both contexts they are two different types of customer because of the different contexts. The question of customer definition is therefore concerned with, first, establishing the groups of individuals or organisations who are customers and clarifying the context in which they use our products or services.

IDENTIFYING CUSTOMER GROUPS

Customer groups can be identified by means of the following three questions which an organisation can ask itself.

Who provides your revenue?

Customers deliver revenue. Using this definition, the logistics company would see the food manufacturer as being its customer. In turn, the food manufacturer would define the retailer as being its customer. A police force would see the government as being its prime customer. A hospital trust would define local authorities, doctors' practices and, perhaps, private health companies as being its customers.

The revenue dimension is a critical one, but not necessarily the most important in terms of strategy. In the case of the logistics company, it is the retailer which drives the supply chain and therefore changes to systems and processes tend to originate from the retailer. The manufacturer then responds to these changes. For the food company, if it is not able to stimulate demand with consumers (who provide revenue to the retailer), then they may lose the interest of their customers as there is little 'pull-through' demand. Similarly, in order to 'add value' to the retailer's business, they need to understand how their product category is bought and consumed in order to advise on demand patterns and promotional opportunities. For these reasons, it would be a mistake for the logistics company to regard the food manufacturer as its sole customer group. We need, therefore, to consider further criteria for identifying the customers who have a role in the strategic development of the business.

Who makes the decision to use your products or services?

There may be situations where the revenue provider does not actually make the purchase decision. In the case of undergraduates attending university, a local authority grant or scholarship may be awarded to provide the revenue for their education, but, often, it is the student who makes the decision as to which university to attend, assuming they are accepted. In healthcare in the UK, a doctor may refer a patient and thereby provide the hospital with revenue. However, in the case of childbirth, the decision as to which hospital to use may be a decision which the parents make, although the hospital's revenue comes from the health authority.

When dealing with a large organisation, different departments may have different roles. In the example of a new sales database, the revenue to acquire the system may be provided by the sales budget, but the decision as to which system to use is made by the information systems group, both areas having different evaluation criteria, and they are therefore distinct customer groups. The notion of the decision-making unit has been a central concept in the marketing of industrial products. The different roles of such a unit are summarised in Figure 4.2.

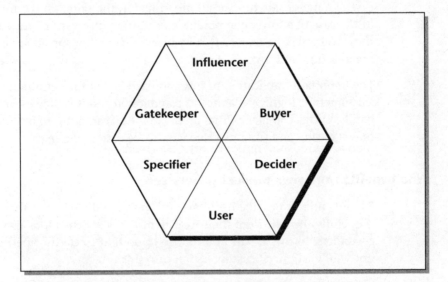

Figure 4.2 Different roles of a decision-making unit in the organisational buying process

The *user* is the individual or group who will ultimately operate or use the product or service. This may be a marketing analyst in the case of an on-line database or a computer operator in the case of a new PC.

The *specifier* sets out the parameters for the generic product or service type to be considered and so this may be a particular technical specification. Some examples of such products or services are generators which are designed to produce a particular range of power outputs, a fleet service which includes all maintenance and the disposal of old cars or simply a straightforward leasing agreement.

The *gatekeeper* role controls the flow of information between potential suppliers and customer organisations. This may be an administrative role, such as a managing director's PA or it may be combined with other roles, such as that of the specifier.

The *influencer* role involves providing other influential inputs. This may take the form of a consultant, brought in to advise on the process or someone else in the organisation who has some relevant knowledge.

The *buyer* is a traditional purchasing role where the buyer establishes a process and set of parameters for the relationship.

The *decider* role is that which makes the final decision to use a particular source of supply. This is likely to be a senior manager in the case of a major purchase or an individual in the purchasing function in the case of a low-value purchase or a straightforward rebuy. All of these roles may be represented by one individual or spread across the organisation and involve significant conflicts and power struggles.

The important implication of this approach is that the definition of 'customers' is highly variable and complicated and it is only by laying hands on this complexity that an organisation can begin to understand how it creates and sustains value with these customer groups.

Who benefits from your product or service?

Patients do not provide hospitals with revenue directly, but they do (hopefully) benefit from their treatment. They are therefore also customers. In this situation, it is also important to clarify whether or not your customers' customers fall into this category.

Companies such as IBM that supply automatic teller machines (ATMs) would regard the banks as their customers. However, it is the banks' customers who benefit. If the ATM manufacturer fails to understand

and respond to this particular customer group, they will ultimately lose their revenue-generating customers – the banks. Similarly, a provider of systems maintenance services, such as ICL Sorbus, may be engaged by an outsourced contractor, such as EDS. EDS is the customer in that it provides the revenue and makes the decision to use the systems maintenance company, but it is EDS's clients which directly benefit from the level of service. They, therefore, need to be given customer status as their views may drive future decisions by EDS.

These ideas can also apply at the intra-organisational level. For example, the facilities services departments of large companies are responsible for the maintenance of buildings, heating, provision of cleaning services, photocopying and fleet management. They have a source of revenue from a central allocation made at Board level, but they also have the other functions of the organisation that benefit from the services they provide. It is the relationship which the facilities departments have with these other departments which will determine their success if, for example, the Board decides to relax the restrictions forcing these other departments to use the facilities services departments' services and allow them to outsource if they so require it.

What these questions achieve

These three questions provide a way of evaluating exactly who your customers are. In many situations, the answer to all three questions can be provided by one group, but, often, they may be separated either within an organisation or else be in totally different organisations.

DEFINING CUSTOMER CONTEXT

Having established the customer groups the organisation needs to focus on, it is also important to clarify the context in which these customers use their particular products or services. For example, a company selling cooking sauces distinguishes between individuals who use the sauce in a planned way, to cut down on the amount of food preparation needed and others who buy in a state of crisis, having realised that they have insufficient ingredients in the house. The latter type of customer is shopping at the last minute and therefore uses alternative retail outlets (convenience stores or garages) and is relatively insensitive to price.

Organisational buying factors, such as urgency and application, mean that the nature of customers and their requirements are quite different. Short-term truck rental customers may be those who regularly experience seasonal peaks in demand and therefore need additional capacity for identifiable short periods, while other customers may experience intermittent demand which is virtually impossible to anticipate and therefore require immediate support at unanticipated times. The customer requirements for a diesel generator will be different if the generator is to operate continuously, supplying constant power, than if the generator is for emergency back-up, only being required in the event of a major power failure.

The issue to be considered here is, strategically, who are the priority customer groups? In what context do they buy and use our products or services? What are the relationships between the groups? Which are the groups which provide the benefits to the organisation outlined in Chapter 1?

One way of addressing these questions is to use the framework outlined in Table 4.1 as a starting point. Here we use as an illustration a prestigious hotel chain to explore some of the potential customer groups we can focus on.

Having identified the customer groups which your organisation is serving, these need to be prioritised in some way so that you can concentrate on those which are of greatest strategic importance to the organisation. For example, in the case of the hotel group, whereas

Table 4.1 Framework for identifying customer groups with a prestigious hotel group being used as an example

Customer groups and contexts	Provide revenue	Make decision	Benefit from product
1 Corporate executives	Sometimes	Sometimes	Directly
2 Corporate travel agents	Yes	Sometimes	Indirectly
3 Corporate travel management companies	Yes	Sometimes	Indirectly
4 Retail travel agents	Yes	Sometimes	Indirectly
5 Incentive organisers	Yes	Yes	Indirectly
6 Independent travellers	Yes	Yes	Yes
7 High-net-worth individuals	Yes	Yes	Yes

independent travellers and high net worth individuals do form an
important part of the business, they are difficult to identify and are
relatively small and fragmented compared to corporate customers
(numbers 1–3) who form a significant proportion of the hotel's
present and future business.

DEFINING WHICH CUSTOMERS ARE STRATEGICALLY IMPORTANT

In order to do this customer attractiveness criteria need to be
established. These will differ from organisation to organisation, but
some of the more common criteria are outlined below.

The size of their business with us

This is the easy one! Assuming we are defining customers on the basis
of the amount of revenue they generate, then it should be relatively
easy to identify those groups which provide a significant proportion
of our revenue.

The Pareto rule of 80 per cent of the revenue being generated by
20 per cent of the customers is often applied to determine which
customers provide the most significant part of the business. For
example, a company manufacturing a food ingredient would identify
its customers as being food manufacturers, the particular ingredient it
manufactures being widely used in puddings and cakes. Many of its
customers are large conglomerates, such as Sara Lee and McVitie's
and, while there are many smaller niche companies to which it sells,
such as local bakeries and a number of distributors and wholesalers,
around 74 per cent of the company's revenue comes from these large
customers, which make up only 18 per cent of its customer base. Is
this the case generally, and are there ways of finding out if it applies
in a particular company?

One way of illustrating the relative power of different parts of the
market is to use the market mapping approach developed by McDonald
and Dunbar,[1] and a brief summary of this approach now follows.

Market mapping involves asking a series of questions about the route
which products or services take from the supplying organisation to
the final consumer. Figure 4.3 shows a market map for a firm which
supplies heating equipment. The five stages in the supply chain are

Manufacturer of product	Distributors	Fitters	Consultants	End-users
AA 42%	BA (National n = 16) 47%	CA (National n = 3) 8%	DA (n = 2000) 10%	EA (Residential (A) n = 600 000) 47%
		CB (Local industries n = 17 500) 50%		
AB 16%	BB (Large industries n = 275) 41%			EB (Residential (B) n = 63 000) 15%
AC 11%		CC (Contractors n = 3500) 35%		EC (Public (A) n = 1800) 20%
AD 9%				
AE 5%	BC (Small industries n = 5500) 11%			ED (Public (B) n = 1800) 2%
AF 17%				
	BD (Superstores n = 9) 1%	CD (Commercial organisations n = 1200) 7%		EE (Commercial n = 45 000) 16%

Supply chain

Figure 4.3 Market map for the total market for heating equipment
Source: based on McDonald and Dunbar[1]

shown, moving from left to right. Each of the five stages is then split into the volume or value of business undertaken by the different players involved in that stage. More sophisticated maps can be drawn to show the different flows of business through different customer groups, but this provides us with a sufficiently detailed starting point.

The first thing which the market mapping process does is to ask a series of questions which are often difficult for organisations to answer. In particular, an organisation may have detailed information about its immediate customers (that is, those which create revenue for the company – in this case, the distributors), but very little understanding of what happens further down the supply chain. While it could be argued that all the supplying companies need to worry about is the distributors, this is a very short-term view. To take a strategic perspective, in order for the supplying companies to be proactive in developing their business with the distributors, they have to understand what is happening further down the supply chain. This can be the only way in which they can anticipate how the market is developing, thereby offering the distributors a value-adding service. If, as the Millennium Report emphasises, organisations have to know what their customers' needs are before their customers know what these are, then part of the understanding necessary to do this is provided by the market map.

It can be seen from the overall map shown in Figure 4.3 that the market is dominated by the national distributors (BA) and the local fitters (CB). This is the overall map, but it is also important to compare the positions of individual companies within this overall picture. Figure 4.4 shows the market map for company AA alone. The pattern for this company is relatively similar to the overall market, although AA is more dependent on the national distributors (BA) and less dependent on the large independent distributors (BB). From the point of view of determining which are presently its strategically important customers, then groups BA and CB would be selected.

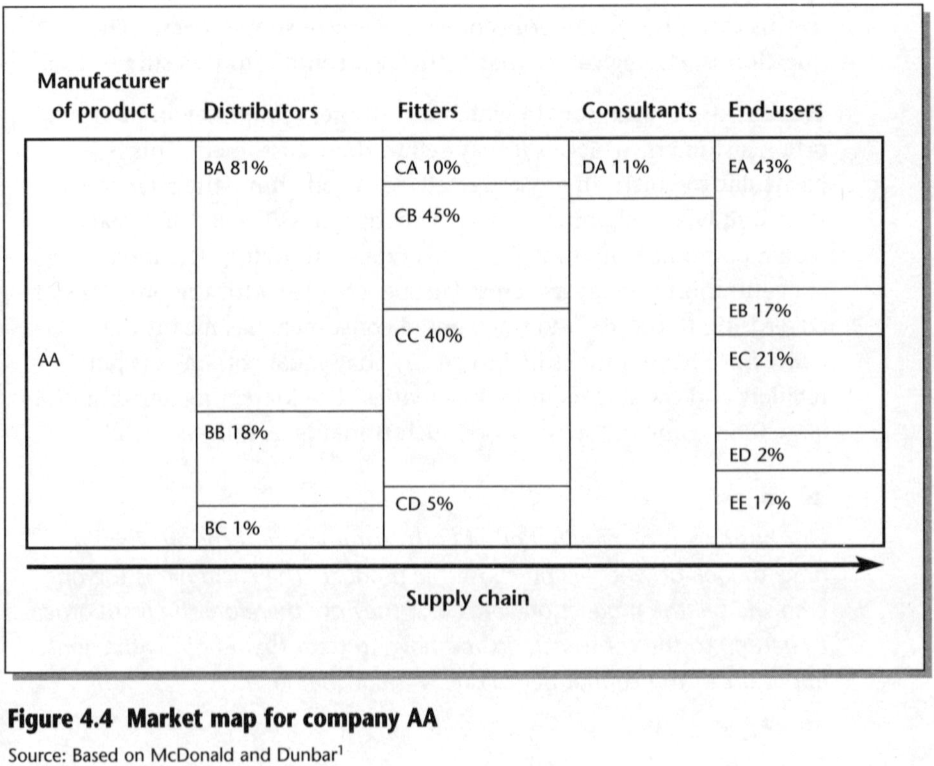

Manufacturer of product	Distributors	Fitters	Consultants	End-users
	BA 81%	CA 10%	DA 11%	EA 43%
		CB 45%		
				EB 17%
		CC 40%		EC 21%
AA	BB 18%			ED 2%
	BC 1%	CD 5%		EE 17%

Supply chain

Figure 4.4 Market map for company AA

Source: Based on McDonald and Dunbar[1]

Their influence over other customer groups

Customers can influence other customer groups in two ways. First, they can be seen to be the market leader in their area and therefore their competitors use them as a benchmark. This seems to be very much the case in the management consultancy business, where a particular initiative is adopted, such as business process reengineering, and a whole industry follows the fashion of having consultants in to reengineer its business. This does not mean, of course, that the consultant who supplies the market leader will get all the potential business, it may, in fact, mean that you do a great service to your competitors by breaking in to one particular organisation, but it may also be that dealing with the market leader makes it easier to get business from those who would not see themselves as a direct rival.

Second, a customer can influence other customers via their suppliers. In the case of a company such as NCR, which develops logistics systems using electronic data interchange (EDI), one key customer may acquire the system and then pressurise or persuade its suppliers to adopt it in order to realise the full benefits of having this system. In this case, the customer becomes the entire supply chain. The question is, strategically, what is the best route into this supply chain.

There is also a third way in which a customer group may influence other customers, which is if they sell to these customers. This is particularly evident in grocery retailing. At one time, the retailer was seen simply as a channel for serving consumers. The last ten years have seen a dramatic shift away from this type of thinking. The increasing concentration of retailers across Europe, coupled with the problems of advertising to diverse and fragmented consumers has meant that companies have restructured to ensure that equal emphasis is put retailers and consumers in their activities. The Marketing Director of a large food company summarised such thinking as follows:

● ● ●

Our business is a combination of both customers and consumers. We have to look at who will purchase the product. The customer is the one who will sell the product onwards and they are therefore the first barrier to getting to the consumer. So you have to treat them both with equal importance. You cannot get to one without the other.

● ● ●

Their stability

Clearly we want to ensure that the customers we focus on are the ones which will, like us, be sustaining performance over the long term. We therefore need to be asking ourselves about our customers' financial configuration and their cash flow. How much time do the management accountants in your organisation spend on assessing the financial stability of your customers? I am not just referring to credit vetting when I ask this question, but to the long-term financial balance of these customers and the implications of this for doing business with them.

The intensity of the competition for them

The notion that the competition for some customers may be less intense than for others is, perhaps, surprising. Everyone is out there fighting for their share of a finite cake, so why might there be less intense competition for some than others.

A software company in the computer-aided design (CAD) sector which requires leading-edge software development and high levels of computing power recently discovered that it, like everyone else, was running around after the big juicy accounts – the large manufacturers, such as car and truck companies. However, very few people were spending a great deal of time on the specialist design houses and other small- to medium-sized enterprises which are involved in various high-technology activities. The industry mindset was focused solely on obtaining the big juicy accounts, thereby maximising sales and minimising marketing costs. This meant that everyone was cutting down on the number of salespeople on the road and moving towards a key account management approach in order to handle the big (remember the Pareto rule) accounts. This particular organisation adopted a different approach, however – deploying a number of regional managers, supported by sector-specific technical support (such as in car design) at head office, along with a dedicated telesales team. By doing this, the company was able to reorientate itself to serve a more fragmented customer group that was largely being neglected by its major competitors, making more cost-effective use of its resources.

The opportunity to offer unique added value

This issue will be explored in more detail later in the book, but it is necessary to consider the implications of it here.

Every organisation has a unique approach to the way it operates which is often difficult for competitors to replicate in the same way. For example, the Disney corporation has a culture which is highly motivated and cohesive and organisations all over the world have attempted to emulate this. Nobody, though, has been able to do it.

If we accept that every organisation is unique, and also that every customer is unique, then the issue here is that of identifying those unique customers who will particularly value your unique way of doing things. For example, Dronningborg Maskinfabrik is a Danish manufacturer of combine harvesters which now supplies all that it produces to Massey Ferguson. The combine harvester business is a global one, with total annual sales of combine harvesters being in the region of 20 000 units (it is around 7000 for western Europe). Dronningborg is one of the smallest manufacturers in this field but it has been at the forefront of innovative design for many years, particularly in its use of electronics. It has developed machines which use X-rays to measure the amount of grain coming into the harvester, which, when linked to a global positioning system, can accurately define the yield at specific points in the field. This information can then be used to calibrate the application of pesticides and fertilisers throughout the year in order to maximise the efficiency of these expensive resources. The type of farmer to whom the Dronningborg can add value is the professional manager who uses integrated computing systems to run the farm and needs this type of information in order to run the business more effectively. The resources and focus of Dronningborg and Massey Ferguson therefore need to be directed at this type of customer profile, as it is in this way that they can add most value.

The opportunity to save costs

The fact that some customers are significantly more costly to serve than others has been a major finding in research into customer retention. In particular, it has been found that retained customers cost less to serve than do new customers.[2] A basic, approximate cost profile for a customer is shown in Figure 4.5.

The reduced costs of retained customers can be explained by a number of factors. First, every new customer creates an acquisition and set-up cost for the organisation. The acquisition cost is the sales cost of acquiring a new customer via sales activity, advertising and so on. The set-up cost is the cost of gearing up to do business with the customer.

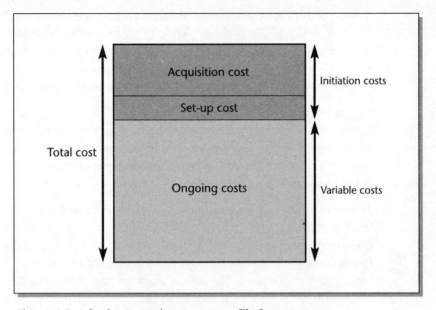

Figure 4.5 A basic, approximate cost profile for a customer

For many industries, customer acquisition costs are particularly high – the cost of salespeople is continually escalating, for example. Direct mail and advertising are also very expensive as, in most industries, the success rate for acquiring new customers by these means is particularly low. For example, a truck distributor estimates that it costs around £2000 to acquire each new customer, whereas the sales effort to renew the fleet of an existing customer cost around half that.

The set-up cost for a new customer can also be high. For insurance policies, the cost of underwriting a new policy is around 10 per cent, whereas the cost of underwriting a renewal policy is around 5 per cent. If an insurance company were able to change the proportion of renewal business from 40 to 80 per cent of its business, this would mean a reduction in its underwriting cost base from 8 to 6 per cent. In other words, it would be able to increase its profitability by 2 per cent for no change in the volume of its sales.

In addition to acquisition and set-up costs, there is some evidence that customers get better at working with you and therefore save you time and effort. This is because they know how to find answers to their queries within your organisation and they can often sort out their problems themselves. This has the result of reducing the ongoing variable costs of doing business with a particular customer.

Indeed, a software company found that, during the first three months after acquiring a new customer, their usage of the telephone hotline was particularly intense. However, after this period, it settled down to a relatively low level. Also, even when the customer then took on a new upgrade, the level of usage of the hotline service was still low.

As you will recall from Chapter 1, von Hippel's notion of customer-focused R&D means that customers become an explicit part of the R&D process, with costs being saved because customers effectively develop and test their own prototypes. These relationships are summarised in Figure 4.6.

These customers are particular types of customers who are at the leading technological edge of their industry. Von Hippel refers to these customers as lead users and describes them as being at the forefront of their chosen industries, with strategies based on continuous innovation. These lead users are customers which organisations in high-tech industries may wish to consider targeting.

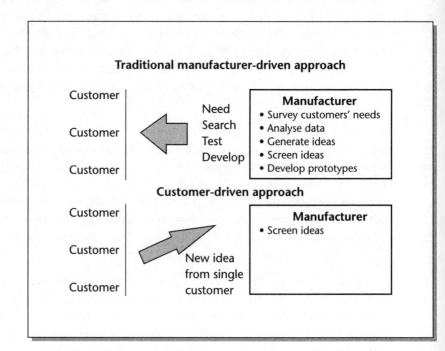

Figure 4.6 The advantages of a customer-driven approach to R&D

Source: Adapted from Eric von Hippel[3]

CONSIDERING THE FUTURE

So far we have based our evaluation on determining those customers who are strategically important today. However, in order to consider the long-term development of the organisation, we need to consider how this may change in the future. Considering the future is not an easy process. In fact, probably the only accurate thing we can say about any long-term forecast is that it will be wrong. While we can perhaps more easily look at market trends to extrapolate volume levels, considering how our customers may change is more problematical.

In considering the 'thinking' aspects of this issue we tend to construct our view of the future based on what has happened in the past. The British motor-cycle industry's view of the future was that the demand for large, noisy motor bikes for enthusiasts would continue. They were wrong. In considering the future, we therefore may need to be more creative than just extrapolating from the past.

Let us use a food manufacturer which makes a number of prepared products based on potatoes, including oven-ready chips and mashed potato, as an example to illustrate this. The company's current market is dominated by the multiple retailers, which make up 80 per cent of its sales. However, a growing segment of its business is moving into the food services sector. This includes fast-food chains, such as Burger King and McDonald's, and the catering services organisations which supply to hotels and restaurants. In this particular sector, margins are less constrained than they are in retailing. Also, these businesses are growing and value- rather than cost-focused. If a new food product such as prepared mashed potato saves them labour costs and allows them to fulfil customer orders more quickly, then the price premium which may be charged is of little consequence. The analysis shown in Table 4.2 illustrates the differences between these two customer groups, both of which are strategically important to the organisation – one on the basis of today's business, the other on tomorrow's.

Although Table 4.2 shows how different customer groups may hold more potential in the future than they do in the present, as discussed in Chapter 2, this is one view and there may be many more alternatives as to how the future will unfold and how different customer groups may become more or less important to the organisation over time. In order to consider some of these alternatives, we need to consider a number of different ways in which our customers could possibly change in the future. This helps us to identify where our assumptions concerning the

Table 4.2 Example of a strategic customer evaluation for a food manufacturer

	Multiple retailers		Food service	
	Now	Future	Now	Future
Size of business	4	4	1	4
Influence over other customers	4	3	2	4
Stability	3	2	3	4
Lack of competition	1	1	3	3
Opportunity to offer added value	2	2	4	4
Opportunity to save costs	3	3	1	3
Totals	17	15	14	22

most attractive customer groups may be challenged so that we can see where the possible threats and opportunities may come from in an uncertain environment.

THE FUTURE POSSIBILITIES FOR CUSTOMERS

When we are thinking about the future, it is only possibilities and their implications that we can reasonably consider. However, these possibilities can provide us with insight and suggest new opportunities and approaches in the way in which we deal with our customers, and the potential which different customer groups may offer. One of the things to come out of the Millennium Report,[4] on which this series of books is based, is that suppliers should be able to know what their customers will need before they do. This is an appropriate ambition, but it is important to rephrase this to embrace the notion that if we just *think* we know what they need, then we are in danger of falling into the old product-led, 'we know best' mindset. The challenge now is to consider the potential divergence of needs and situations which customers will face in the future. This places the organisation in a better position to respond quickly to the new signals which represent a shift in customer demand.

In order to see how we might set about meeting customers' needs in this way, we will apply a development of the scenario technique outlined by Peter Schwartz in his excellent book.[5] Figure 4.7 shows the rationale for applying an approach which considers multiple possibilities, such as scenarios, to our strategic thinking. As discussed in Chapter 2, one of the pathologies of strategic thinking is the narrow-minded myopia which limits the interpretations of the trends and developments in the environment and also reduces the likelihood of considering more than one response with any degree of seriousness. The case for the scenario approach is that it combines the strengths of a multifocus perspective, by considering multiple scenarios, with a single-focus view of a particular future in each scenario.

There are many permutations of the scenario process, but the following is an approach which has been found to be particularly useful when specifically considering customers. While the scenario process can be quite complicated and demanding, it delivers a number of positive outcomes, which can be intended or emergent. The six basic stages in the development and application of customer-based scenarios are now outlined and then the kinds of benefits this process can deliver are discussed.

1 Identify customer group and context

It is important that the process moves from a clear start point. If it is not sufficiently focused, this will start to be seen because the following stages become more difficult to achieve. Thus it is necessary to have quite a specific definition of the customer group and the

	Single-focus view	Multi-focus view
Strengths	• Focus • Clarity • Commitment • Communication	• Facilitative • Keeps minds open
Weaknesses	• Myopic • False impression of certainty	• Creates confusion • Difficult to guide actions • Unable to achieve consensus

Figure 4.7 The rationale for scenario development

buying context. For example, if the scenarios started with 'the financial services market', this would be too broad a definition from which to develop a clear understanding of the driving forces and their interrelationships. If, however, we use 'pension provision for the self-employed', then we have a very specific focus which will enable us to explore the factors at work with real clarity. The implications are that specific groups of scenarios need to be applied to a number of differing customer groups. While this involves a lot of commitment, it is the only way to achieve real insights into the possible ways in which this customer group may develop in the future.

2 Identify drivers for change

Having defined the customer group, the next step is to identify the factors which may change the way in which these customers behave in the future. The simple PEST (Political/legal, Economic, Sociological/cultural and Technological) checklist may be one way of doing this. The trick is to keep it clearly focused on what might change the way in which the customers will buy your product or service. There is always a danger that this exercise becomes too broad and ends up developing into a series of global scenarios, rather than a set of scenarios which give specific insights into your customers and your products and services. It is important that this stage is done well as, again, it will affect the quality of subsequent analysis.

3 Sort drivers based on outcomes

Having arrived at a list of driving forces, these can now be sorted into the different types of outcomes which can be expected. Put all the forces you have identified under two headings. First, 'Certain'. Put all the forces which are considered to have a single outcome which is obvious and inevitable under this heading. For example, in the case of provision of care for the elderly it can be relatively certain that, demographically, the average age in Europe is increasing.

Be careful that you do not have too many driving forces in this category as, in many situations, it is the factors which appear, on the face of it, to be certain which cause the biggest upsets. The 'Certain' category should therefore contain the predetermined factors which we already know about and are therefore already established in our mindset.

The important question is which are the forces that will make a difference because they are less certain? Thus, the second list is entitled 'Uncertain'. For this exercise, list under this heading all the forces which have a number of different potential outcomes. Having done the list, it is useful to show the uncertain driving forces using an onion diagram, like that illustrated in Figure 4.8 which shows such forces for a strategy consultancy firm considering its base of medium-sized business units. The core of the onion is the focal issue. The middle ring holds the uncertain driving forces and the outer one the alternative outcomes which have been defined. For example, one of the driving forces affecting the consultancy operation is the clients' attitudes to risk. Here we consider the possibilities that this may become more *laissez-faire* or that there is greater accountability in response to a more conservative attitude to risk.

4 The importance of driving forces

Once the lists have been developed, identify the most important of the uncertain driving forces to work on – that is, those which are most influential in bringing about change to the customer group. Do not spend huge amounts of time agonising as to whether a driving force is ranked one or two. It will be difficult to make very fine judgements, but three or four driving forces will clearly emerge as the most important.

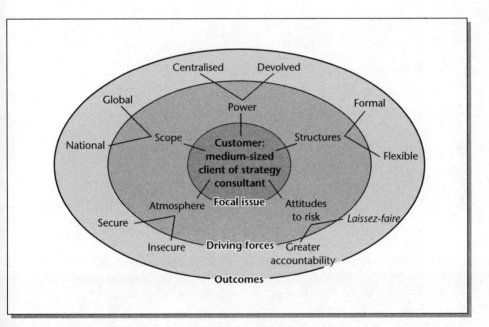

Figure 4.8 Using an onion diagram to illustrate the uncertain outcomes of a strategy consultancy customer's attitudes to risk

5 Creating the scenarios

Starting with the driving force which you ranked as the most important, take the first outcome and develop a causal map by asking the following questions.

- What will cause this particular outcome?
- What will be the effects of this outcome?

Using the example of the strategy consulting practice, a causal map for the outcome of 'greater accountability' from the driving force 'attitude to risk' is illustrated in Figure 4.9. The causal map shows a series of concepts, shown as text, which are linked in terms of cause and effect by arrows. Below the dotted line we can see that a number of higher level factors are causing this outcome based on the autonomy of senior managers to make judgements. Above the dotted line we can see some of the effects of this outcome, culminating in an increased threat of litigation.

Having undertaken this exercise for the most important uncertain driving force, work round the outer ring of the onion diagram to identify any other outcomes which are compatible with the elements in this causal map – in this case, those which are compatible with

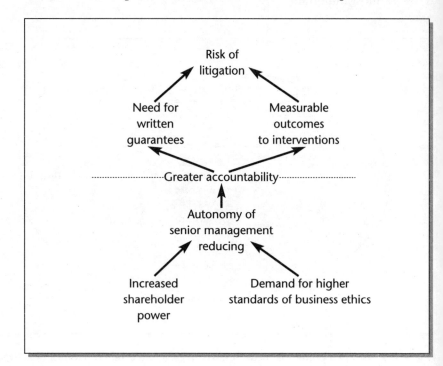

Figure 4.9 Causal map of the outcome 'greater accountability'

greater accountability. The purpose of the causal mapping exercise is to elaborate the outcome to gain a greater understanding of how it may interact with other outcomes. Referring back to Figure 4.8, it seems that the outcomes 'insecure' (driving force = 'atmosphere') and 'formal' (driving force = 'structures'), 'centralised' (driving force = 'power') and 'global' (driving force = 'scope') are compatible with the issues raised in Figure 4.9. In this example, all the driving forces are being applied, but it may be that, at times, no other driving forces outcome links to the most important uncertain driving force, in which case we would repeat the exercise for the second most important and subsequent rankings until we feel that we have linked together most of the important outcomes. Bringing these outcomes together gives us the basis for establishing the scenarios. In the example, we have two scenarios. Scenario 1 is where clients are under pressure to be highly accountable to stakeholders. This creates an atmosphere of insecurity, with highly formalised reporting lines and centralised control. Scenario 2 is the converse, with a more relaxed and flexible management team, its members having the autonomy to sort out their own issues in their own way.

6 Using the scenarios

This is perhaps the least well discussed and most important part. As a basis for considering the application of scenarios, we have expanded the example to define the scenarios and to explore the implications they have for the business and to consider the driving forces which may create these particular scenarios. Figures 4.10 and 4.11 show how this may be applied to our example of the strategy consultant's client.

Scenarios are not an end in themselves – they have a number of important outcomes. These are summarised below in terms of content and process.

The benefits of scenarios: content

Identifying key signals in the environment

Identifying the signals in the environment which suggest a particular course of events is evolving. For example, if we were to use the ideas from Figure 4.9, this might mean an increase in regulations on corporate governance, an increased consolidation of ownership, with major corporations having a strong influence in their small subsidiaries. The importance of the scenario is that it alerts us to the logic which might cause a particular series of events to unfold should this happen.

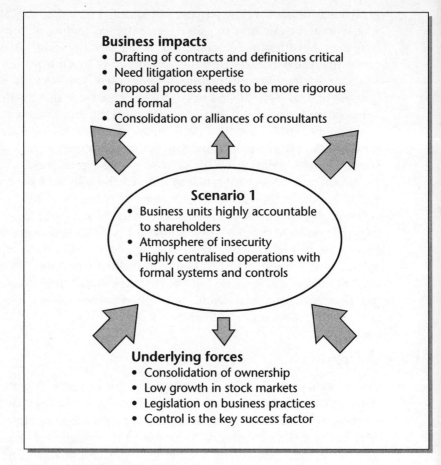

Figure 4.10 The implications of scenario 1

Identifying the potential for longer-term 'seed-setting' activities

In scenario 1 (see Figure 4.10), the suggestion of an alliance or group of consultants who would share their expertise and risk on litigation may be one area which could be explored in a low-key way. These types of relationships take time to build, so if conversations on this topic are started, this could give the organisation an advantage if things begin to move in this particular direction. Similarly, for scenario 2 (see Figure 4.11), the need to develop creativity could be met by means of a number of initiatives and processes, such as setting aside days for the consultants to explore new techniques and ideas. Again this is a relatively low-key move, but, like the previous example, is an activity which could yield benefits in the long run.

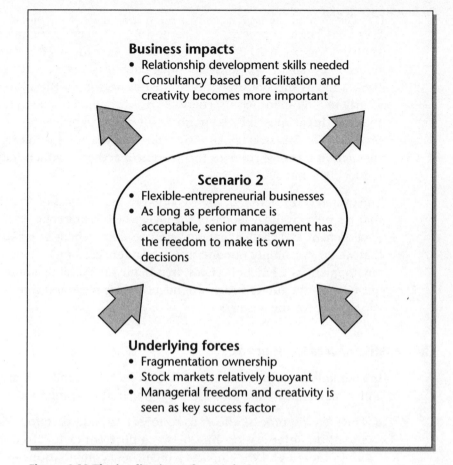

Figure 4.11 The implications of scenario 2

Identifying strengths and weaknesses relative to the competition

The two scenarios we have just been discussing help to clarify where, in relation to the current basis of competition, different firms may be able to achieve success, or are likely to struggle, in these different situations. Here, the basis for success in these two scenarios would be to have a strong holding company which has the litigation expertise needed, but with the business unit being a small, creative organisation which is given plenty of autonomy. The basis for failure would be for it to become a relatively small organisation which is conservative and set in its ways, making it unlikely to add value via increased creativity. It would also be particularly vulnerable to the threats posed in scenario 1.

Evaluating strategies

Scenarios can be a powerful way of testing the viability of a chosen strategy. For example, if the strategy defined by the organisation is to become a small, specialist boutique emphasising creativity and facilitation as the key strengths of the business, then the strategy is clearly in alignment with scenario 2. However, it also illustrates that the threats posed by scenario 1 will create significant problems for this strategy and, therefore, they require thinking through in terms of some of the actions or activities which may reduce their impact.

The overall contribution of the scenario process in terms of content is that we are considering some of the logic which creates our environment and challenging our priorities and agendas to make sure that we are not simply responding to the future customer environment as a function of past trends, but are building and testing out views of the future which will help generate ideas and consolidate the strategy for the business.

The benefits of scenarios: process

In addition to the above, the scenario process has a number of benefits which may improve the processes occurring in the organisation.

- The scenario process allows us to reflect on, and therefore learn about, the interrelationships between different factors in the environment and the impacts which these combinations may have. This relates to the concept of alignment,[6] where a change in the customer environment only happens when a particular series of variables come together. For example, a change in our desire to know about the contents of food products is driven by a concern over food safety, but also by increased access to information on this subject via the media and the Internet. Understanding and learning from such interrelationships will allow us to become more responsive to the potential changes in the environment.

- The process of creating scenarios forces us to leave the here and now of day-to-day routine and seriously absorb ourselves in the future. This is a key element of strategic thinking – developing the 'helicopter view', rising above the trees and seeing where we should be heading.

- Scenarios can also help in the development of a common language within the organisation for referring to the future and considering its implications. Scenarios are a shorthand for the complexity of the environment. Talking about the concepts at work in them gives us a basis for introducing this complexity into our day-to-day thinking.

- Scenarios can also be facilitative in that they can help generate commitment to future change. By using the process, groups throughout the organisation can begin to explore the implications of the changing environment. One of the key problems in the change process is that of instilling a recognition of the need for change. Scenarios can be a powerful aid in bringing this awareness about (we discuss the concept of customer-focused change more fully in Chapter 7).

CUSTOMER SCENARIOS: AN EXAMPLE

In order to ensure that the scenario process is clearly understood, we shall now work through an example. This example is based on the grocery retail sector in the UK.[7] The implications drawn from the process are intended to guide a grocery retailer in considering some of the strategic issues which may bring about change in its customer base.

Stage 1: The focal issue

The focal issue requires a clear definition of the customer type and the context we are considering. In this case, we take an average middle-class family of two adults and two children and consider their primary weekly shop (Figure 4.12). We could alternatively have considered single professional people or looked at the 'top-up' shop which is often made to supplement the main shopping trip.

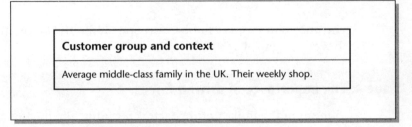

Customer group and context

Average middle-class family in the UK. Their weekly shop.

Figure 4.12 Defining the focal issue

Stages 2, 3 and 4: Identifying driving forces and categorising them as being either certain or uncertain and ranking the uncertain factors in order of importance (by their impact on the way the customer buys).

CERTAIN (forces for change)	
Driving force	**Outcome**
Demographics	Older population, trend towards having children later
Food awareness	More awareness of food chain

UNCERTAIN (forces for change)			
Driving force	**Outcome 1**	**Outcome 2**	**Rank**
Attitude to food	Food safety paramount	Apathy	1
Buyer affluence	Affluent	Economically restricted	3
Attitude to technology	Internet aware	Return of the Luddities	6
Society	Polarised: us and them	Common good	7
Employment	Job security	Job insecurity	5
Mobility	Car-based society grows	Public transport	2
Buyer situation	Time limited	Time limitless	4

Figure 4.13 Finding the driving forces, categorising them as 'certain' or 'uncertain', then ranking the uncertain factors in order of importance

The uncertain factors can be incorporated into the onion diagram, shown in Figure 4.14.

Stage 4: The importance of driving forces

In terms of the impact of the factors regarding the buying of groceries, the most important is identified as being 'attitude to food', followed by 'mobility' of buyers, followed by 'buyer affluence'.

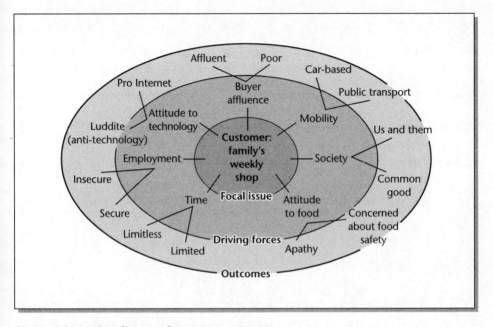

Figure 4.14 Onion diagram for grocery customer

Whether or not these are in a 'correct' order is less important than that we start focusing on those factors which we regard as being the most important.

Stage 5: Developing the scenarios

Having established the order of importance, we create a causal map of the first driving force and the first outcome. In this case, the factor is 'attitude to food' with the outcome being 'concerned about food safety'. This is illustrated in Figure 4.15.

The next stage is to move round the outer onion ring to see if any of the other outcomes appear to be compatible with the elements in the causal map for the 'concerned about food safety' outcome. The connections made are summarised in Figure 4.16, which shows the extended causal map, the new elements having been added in.

As shown in Figure 4.16, two further outcomes can be linked in to the causal map for the driving force 'concerned about food safety'. The map has enabled us to see linkages between these elements. In this case, we have a situation where an increase in food-related disease, combined with a high level of affluence and awareness, led to a customer base which is switching its allegiances to particular sources

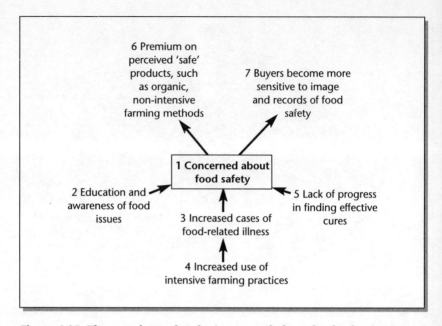

Figure 4.15 The causal map for the 'concerned about food safety' outcome

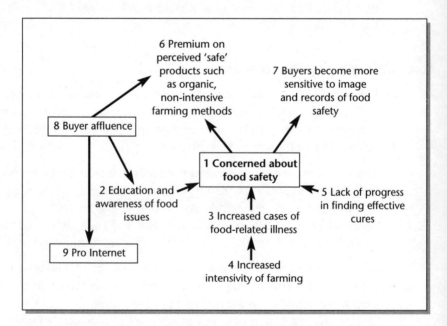

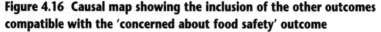

Figure 4.16 Causal map showing the inclusion of the other outcomes compatible with the 'concerned about food safety' outcome

of food. The converse scenario is where a relatively ignorant customer base is less responsive to these issues, either because there is no increase in disease or because they see food choice as being less of a factor in avoiding these diseases.

Having used this driving force to develop some preliminary ideas, we move on to consider the next-ranked factor, which is to do with mobility, the first outcome of which to be considered is a 'car-based society' (see Figure 4.17).

Once we have undertaken a preliminary assessment of the drivers and consequences of a 'car-based society' for the grocery sector, we can then consider which other outcomes in the outer ring of Figure 4.14 are compatible with this. These are shown in Figure 4.18.

Having undertaken this analysis, a number of conclusions emerge. First, 'buyer affluence' impacts on both of the driving forces we have identified, indicating that it is an underlying factor in both the scenarios. Second, there are implications around the time-based issues raised which may also link with job insecurity. For example, people are working longer hours in multiple jobs and this places particular constraints on their shopping.

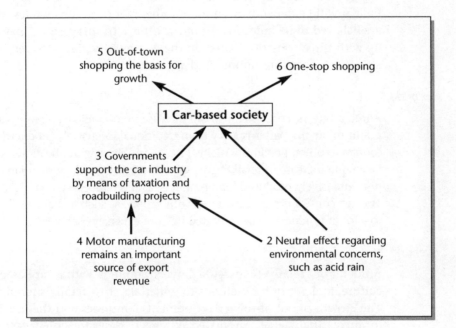

Figure 4.17 Causal map for the outcome of a 'car-based society'

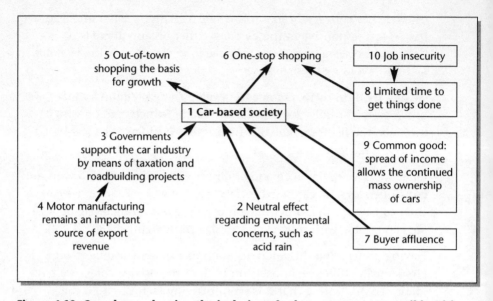

Figure 4.18 Causal map showing the inclusion of other outcomes compatible with that of 'car-based society'

In order to continue to develop the scenarios, we would repeat these iterations in order to clarify some of the main distinctive themes which allow us to develop the scenarios. The number of scenarios we look at will be dependent on the number of groups of variables which are believed to be independent of the others. In this case we may end up with three scenarios, based on the dominant variable 'buyer affluence'. These are summarised as follows.

Scenario 1

Affluent buyers, combined with an increase in food-related disease, cause a shift in buying patterns away from traditional intensively produced food sources to other, previously niche, lines of supply. The implications would be a rapid increase in retail chains specialising in organic, vegetarian or non-intensively produced food products (as has happened in the USA). The key constraints are concerned with supply, as such a change will lead to a lot of products being imported in from expensive sources.

Scenario 2

Affluent, but relatively insecure, buyers, combine with a car-based culture, look for quick methods to undertake their family shopping. The growth of out-of-town developments continues and the race is on for increasingly large, automated systems in order to achieve fast through-put in stores.

Scenario 3

Buyers who are increasingly concerned about their financial limitations become increasingly price-sensitive. Concerns about the ingredients of food products is falling and there is also a rise in consumption of highly processed foods, leading to a move away from fresh products. Car ownership is falling and the increased reliance on public transport is shifting shopping patterns to city centres and residential sites where small, modular discount sheds are developing to sell commodity-based items.

Stage 6: Using the scenarios

Each of the three scenarios is summarised in Figures 4.19, 4.20 and 4.21. The important implications of these scenarios are that they help to identify some of the potential driving forces, but they also suggest some of the different issues which the business may have to take account of in terms of what the norms for serving these customers may become.

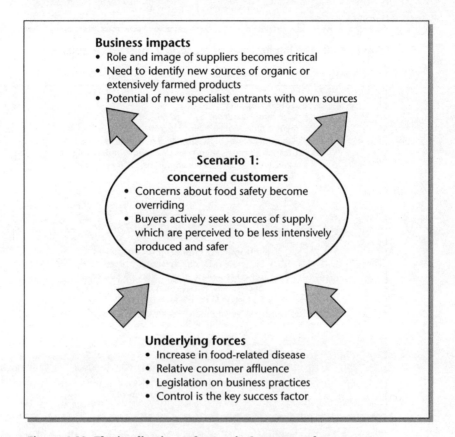

Figure 4.19 The implications of scenario 1: concerned consumers

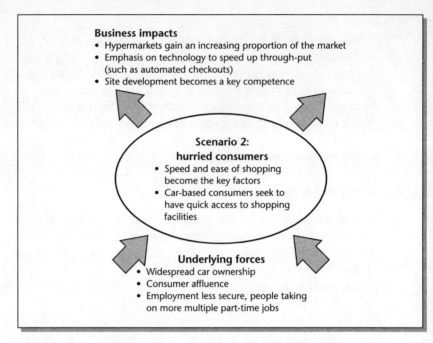

Figure 4.20 The implications of scenario 2: hurried consumers

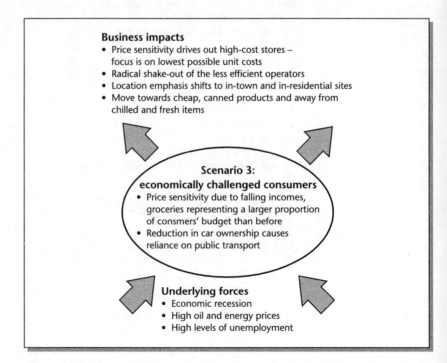

Figure 4.21 The implications of scenario 3: economically challenged consumers

Table 4.3 indicates some of the potential responses and interpretations of these three distinct scenarios. For example, the types of signals which would be expected in the environment if a particular scenario was developing, some of the seed-setting activities which may be undertaken at a relatively low cost now, to explore the implications of some of these scenarios and a consideration of the different aspects of the business which may become strengths and weaknesses in these different scenarios.

The important point to emphasise from Table 4.3 is that it is not simply a case of picking the scenario you want and building around that, but, rather, of exploring the different possibilities which may exist. The purpose of the scenarios is not to tell you what the future *will* be, but to explore the different *potential* futures and to ask what these mean for

Table 4.3 Exploring the implications of the scenarios

Implications	Scenario 1: concerned	Scenario 2: hurried	Scenario 3: challenged
Signals expected in the environment	Increased incidence of food-related disease and media attention, increased consumer awareness of food-related disease issues	Legislation and planning around the car, greater part-time employment, higher job turnover	Recessionary pressures, increasing energy costs, reducing employment levels
Seed-setting activities	Explore alternative supply routes, identify potential alliances	Initiate to improve customer through-put, develop planning concepts and potential sites	Initiate unit cost projects, acquire interest in local store groups
Strengths and weaknesses	S = 'alternative sources of supply', high-quality image W = dependence on suppliers of intensively produced foods poor-quality image and dependence on 'fresh' products	S = out-of-town sites with high traffic potential, one-stop shop formats	S = discounter, cost-efficient ethos, low marketing costs W = high-cost outlets and big marketing spend

the organisation. There may well be responses which would be appropriate in a number of different situations. For example, unit cost efficiencies and the ability to develop and sustain alliances. These kinds of outcomes, which challenge and explore the basis of success, are the benefits of the process of developing customer scenarios.

In this chapter, we have considered three areas regarding customers. First, definition. We need to have a clear idea as to which customer groups we are aiming at. These are often assumed to be self-evident, but, in reality, every organisation has a multitude of customer groups and may not have given them much thought. The hard part is the second area – determining which of these various disparate groups are fundamental to the strategic development of the business. The third area is considering the possible futures these customers may experience and the issues which these possibilities raise for the organisation.

KEY SUMMARY POINTS

1 Identifying exactly who your customers are can be both difficult and challenging, but knowing who they are is fundamental to ensuring that the business is focusing on the right groups of customers.

2 Customers can be defined using three distinct criteria:
   - whether or not they generate revenue for the organisation,
   - whether or not they make the decision to acquire a particular product or service,
   - whether or not they benefit from the product or service.

3 In addition to knowing the characteristics of our customers, it is important that we relate these to the buying context. This gives more clarity to our understanding of how the customers are behaving in that specific context.

4 Organisations very rarely have only one customer group to deal with – most have a myriad of customers – and the challenge is to identify which groups require most strategic attention.

5 We determine which customers are important to us by looking at:
   - the value of the business they provide,
   - their influence over other customers,
   - how stable their business is,
   - the competitive intensity that relates to serving them,
   - whether or not there is an opportunity for the supplier to offer something unique to this customer

- the opportunity the customer offers for saving costs.

6 The customers who are strategically important now, may not be the ones who will be important to us in the future.

7 Developing customer-based scenarios provides an opportunity to:

- pick up key strategic signals from the environment (forces which may create change in customer behaviour),
- identify seed-setting actions which can be undertaken to build for the future,
- explore the strengths and weaknesses of your organisation and competitors,
- evaluate your chosen strategy.

KEY QUESTIONS AND DIAGNOSTICS

Without referring to any other information, can you list the key customer groups for your organisation?

On what criteria do you decide to prioritise your customers? Compare these with the criteria given in this chapter.

Write down the three most important customer groups for your organisation. What are the external events which would make these customers very profitable to do business with? Consider the external events which would make these customers disastrous for the organisation. What does this tell you?

CUSTOMER IDENTITY DIAGNOSTIC

Score each of these statements in terms of how strongly you agree or disagree with them. Add up the scores and see what your total means.

	Agree			Disagree	
In our organisation, we have no clear idea of who all our customers are.	1	2	3	4	5
We know exactly what is going to happen to our customers in the future.	1	2	3	4	5
There will be no change in the types of customers which are important to our business.	1	2	3	4	5
We rarely make changes to the way we do things.	1	2	3	4	5
We frequently reappraise our whole customer base and consider what our ideal customers should look like.	5	4	3	2	1
You will never get our salespeople to consider different types of customers.	1	2	3	4	5
There is no point in thinking too far ahead with regard to customers – they will always tell us what we need to do.	1	2	3	4	5

> **Score**
>
> 25–35: A proactive approach to customer identity is alive and well.
>
> 15–25: There is evidence of life, but not as we'd like it, Jim.
>
> 0–15: High level of apathy. If this does not change, the organisation is unlikely to develop or even survive.

SUGGESTED FURTHER READING

Abell, D. F. (1980), *Defining the Business: The Starting Point of Strategic Planning*, Englewood Cliffs, NJ, Prentice-Hall. This is a useful overview of how a business may go about defining its diverse groups of customers.

Van der Heijden, K. (1996), *Scenarios: The Art of Strategic Conversation*, Chichester, John Wiley. A very comprehensive and concise overview of the application of scenarios in organisations.

REFERENCES

[1] McDonald, M., and Dunbar, I. (1995), *Market Segmentation*, Basingstoke, Macmillan

[2] Reichheld, F. F., and Sasser, W. E., Jr. (1990), 'Zero Defections: Quality Comes to Services', *Harvard Business Review*, 68 (September/October) 105–11

[3] Von Hippel, Eric, (1978), 'Successful Industrial Products from Customer Ideas', *Journal of Marketing*, January, 39–49

[4] 'Management Development to the Millenium' Institute of Management, July 1994

[5] Schwartz, P. (1991), *The Art of the Long View*, New York, Doubleday

[6] Grundy, A. N. (1992), *Corporate Strategy and Financial Decisions*, London, Kogan Page

[7] I would like to thank Julie Verity for her help in developing this example.

CHOOSING AND DEFINING CUSTOMER STRATEGIES

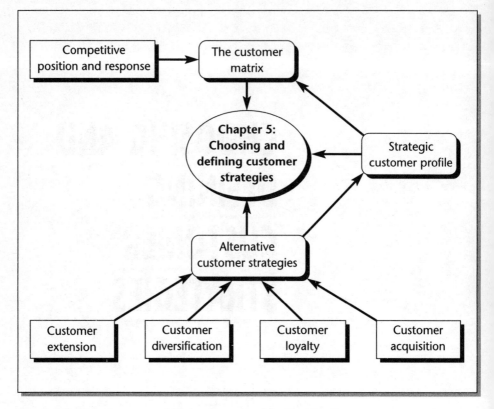

Figure 5.1 Overview map of the areas covered in Chapter 5

In this chapter we consider the potential directions or strategies which can be adopted by an organisation in terms of the customers it seeks to serve in the future. The content of the chapter is summarised in Figure 5.1.

The subjects discussed here can be gathered under three broad headings:

- the direction of customer strategies, which considers some of the alternative routes which can be taken to develop the organisation and its relationship with its customers
- the focus of customer strategies, which is concerned with the strategic customer profiles which will provide the focal point for strategic thinking
- the positioning of customer strategies, which is concerned with the location of the organisation on Cliff Bowman's 'customer matrix'.[1]

THE DIRECTION OF CUSTOMER STRATEGIES

A well-established framework for considering market strategies is the Ansoff matrix. Introduced by Igor Ansoff in his book *Corporate Strategy* in 1965,[2] this framework is still very much alive in business school curriculums and management texts. The Ansoff matrix is summarised in Figure 5.2.

If our level of analysis is concerned with customers, rather than markets, then this framework is too broad to enable us to be clear about the direction we are taking. For example, if we follow a market penetration strategy, does this mean that we are selling more to existing customers or the same to new customers in a particular market? These are two distinct strategies which each require a different emphasis. Does market development mean that we are focusing on new customers in new markets or do our existing customers also operate in these new markets?

In order to provide a framework which allows the focus on the customer to be maintained, the Ansoff matrix is adapted by redefining the contents of the boxes. This revised framework is termed the customer growth matrix and is shown in Figure 5.3.

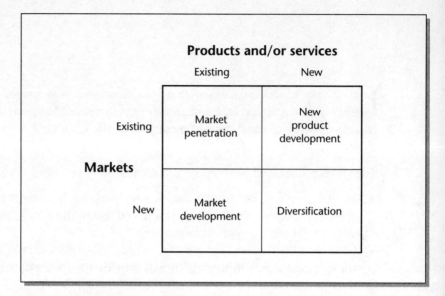

Figure 5.2 The Ansoff matrix[2]

The customer growth matrix illustrates four distinct strategies by which the organisation can grow, establishing particular relationships with customers (growth may be defined as profit, revenues or increases in any other criteria which are used to judge performance).

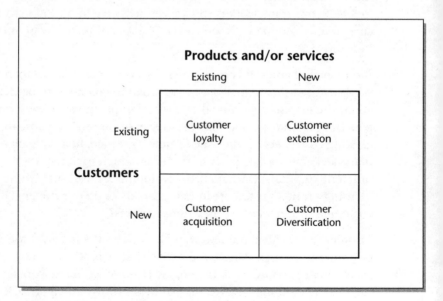

Figure 5.3 The customer growth matrix

Customer loyalty strategies

Much has already been written about customer loyalty strategies and their application to a wide range of businesses.[3] Here we shall draw on some of the fundamental principles which make this the starting point for any customer-based strategy. Increased customer loyalty has been found to generate increased profitability from a number of sources. First, there is empirical evidence that loyal customers tend to spend a greater amount with you over time, they act as referral agents, thereby bringing you new customers and, finally, they may also cost less to serve than new customers. These factors combine to provide strong evidence that organisational profitability is directly linked to the loyalty of its customers (as illustrated in Figure 5.4) and that we should focus our strategies on increasing customer retention, rather than on acquiring greater market share. Figure 5.4 illustrates the point that effort applied in increasing the average customer loyalty lifetime from 3 to 5 years could have a significantly greater impact on profitability than would moving market share from 30 to 40 per cent.

These are, of course, generalisations and do not apply to every business context. However, the question is more about which customers provide these benefits than customers *per se*. Frederick Reichheld talks about having the 'right customers'. If an organisation has the right customers it has an instant competitive advantage.

A customer loyalty strategy is the basis for sustaining competitive advantage. It is also true that loyalty programmes are not appropriate if you do not have the right customers. For example, when entering new geographic markets, the business may initially be based on smaller groups of perhaps less risk-averse customers in order to get established. However, strategically speaking, the objective may be not to develop long-term relationships with these customers, but to shift the customer profile over time in order to fit with the strategic objectives and it would be then that a loyalty programme would be set up.

Customer extension strategies

Customer extension strategies are often used in conjunction with customer loyalty programmes. They are concerned with maintaining the relationships the business has already with its customers, but develop it further by offering a wider range of products and services. Many professional service firms – such as the big six accountancy firms – have based their strategies on their ability to extend their relationships with their clients into new products and services. This has been the basis on which the Virgin group has operated. Whether

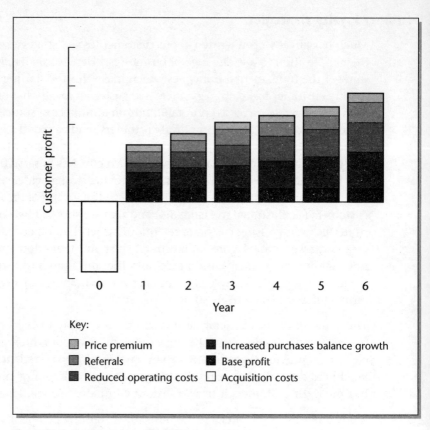

Figure 5.4 Customer profitability over time
Source: Based on Reichheld[4]

it be retailing music, flying across the Atlantic or financial services, the Virgin brand is aimed at a particular type of customer. The strategy Richard Branson is following is to build on this relationship by offering many different products and services, all tailored to this customer group. The growth in financial services that are offered through retail stores is another example of where greater returns are derived from customer extension strategies.

Such extension strategies have caused industry or market definitions to become more and more fuzzy. Organisations in previously distinct areas of the market are now competing for the same customers and meeting the same customer needs by means of these strategies. In the area of management consultancy, firms are able to offer their clients an increasingly wider variety of services which include information systems, personal development and outplacement, organisational image development, advice on ethical positioning and so forth. At one level this can be seen as a form of product development, but it is, in fact, driven by a clear focus on existing customers and the opportunities they provide for revenue and profit.

Customer acquisition strategies

Customer acquisition strategies apply where there is a need to change the existing profile by acquiring more appropriate customers. This is necessary, for example, when the business is operating in a rapidly growing market or when there is some particular requirement to grow rapidly, perhaps in order to realise greater economies of scale and experience than the competition. In these latter cases, the emphasis may be on obtaining new customers, but they need to be similar to existing customers.

Customer acquisition strategies may make a lot of sense if the existing customer base can play a role in recruiting new customers. Many small businesses develop because they are able to secure one high-profile customer and then that customer generates further business from other customers. While the high-profile customer may not be the most profitable in terms of the costs of doing business with them, they are worth having because they enable the business to acquire other more profitable customers, who see the patronage of the high-profile customer as an indication of the suppliers' ability to provide high-quality products and services.

Customer diversification strategies

Customer diversification strategies involve the highest risk as they involve developing business with new customers using new products and services. It is highly unlikely that this is a feasible strategy for an organisation to follow unless there are particular opportunities, such as new technology or processes, or the availability of a partner which can bring its own customer base or expertise into play in making the new strategy work.

The greatest value of mentioning this category here, however, is to show that this is not always the logical, low-risk strategy it appears to be. Let us take as an example a company owned by a large multinational conglomerate which specialised in electrical connectors. Historically, its customer base was large aircraft manufacturers operating in the aerospace market – mainly those specialising in military applications. The reforms in the former Soviet Union and changes in military expenditure world-wide led the company to believe that it should look elsewhere to secure its future growth. As the company manufactured electrical connectors, it decided to move into making connectors for the white goods industry (cookers, fridges and so on) and built another plant to manufacturer such connectors. In this case, the customers were not in fact the white goods manufacturers, but, rather, various distributors that supplied components of original equipment and spare parts to such manufacturers. These distributors required a wholly different level of service. The company's sales teams were used to dealing with slow-moving, bureaucratic military organisations and so found it very difficult to meet the demands of the new customer base. In addition, the production technology involved in making these new connectors proved more difficult to operate efficiently than had been envisaged and, in the end, the organisation had to be rescued by the holding company, at the cost of most of the organisation's senior management team. In this case, a customer diversification strategy had been entered into without sufficient research and so the organisation was trying to cope with radically different customers and new product technology at the same time.[5]

Combining different customer strategies

The differing strategic options we have been looking at can be summarised as shown in Figure 5.5. Combined strategies of loyalty through extension and acquisition by means of customer referrals illustrate how loyalty can be used as a basis for developing a growth strategy.

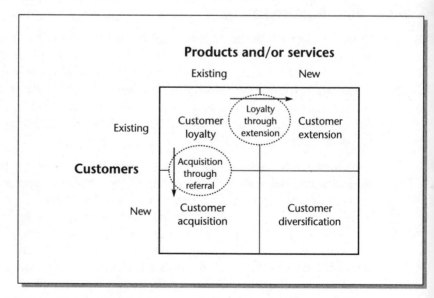

Figure 5.5 Combining elements of the customer growth matrix

In order to begin to clarify where the real basis for sustainable competitive advantage is, we need to gain further clarity and focus regarding the strategically important customer groups and their needs. To do this, we introduce the concept of the strategic customer profile.

THE FOCUS OF CUSTOMER STRATEGIES –
CREATING A STRATEGIC CUSTOMER PROFILE

A large part of the rationale for this book is that we need to shift the emphasis in strategic thinking away from markets and towards customers. The dilemma we face is the tension between the simplicity of markets and the complexity of customers. Markets are an aggregated output of the relationship between customers and products. They therefore provide us with a clear understanding of the nature and scope of the opportunity. However, they do not provide us with a clear focus on where sustainable competitive advantage can be achieved. Ultimately, in order to do this, we need to consider each customer individually to maximise the value we are offering. However, this is not practical, so we need a mechanism by means of which we can bring specific customer issues into the strategy process. The mechanism used here is the strategic customer profile.

The importance of the strategic customer profile is that it promotes thought as to what the optimal customer may be like and therefore we can clarify how exactly we can uniquely add value to what we are offering customers or how we can serve them at lower cost, thereby gaining sustainable competitive advantage. The distinction between a strategic customer profile and 'the market' is that they operate at different levels of analysis. Markets, as we have seen, are an aggregation and so are useful for getting a sense of proportion and scope – particularly in terms of making choices between different markets – but *because* they are aggregated they do not tell us how particular customers behave. Strategic customer profiles, on the other hand, represent particular groups and contexts and therefore lend more clarity to our strategic thinking.

For example, if the organisation is following a customer loyalty strategy, then the strategic customer profile will represent the existing customer base and, more specifically, those existing customers we consider will provide the greatest set of benefits for the lowest cost. If a customer acquisition strategy is being followed, then the strategic customer profile will represent those customers we are seeking to acquire. If the strategy is based on acquisition through referral, then we need to focus on both the existing customers most likely to provide referrals and the new customers we are seeking to acquire. The strategic customer profile is therefore concerned with the groups of customers we see as being central to the development of the organisation. This is our intention, so they are an intended focus for the organisation.

The customer profile therefore clarifies our intended customer groups. These should be made quite specific in order to send a clear signal about where the priorities of the organisation lie. The criteria used to define the customer profile will vary because of the need to pick out the particular factors on which the organisation can build competitive advantage. However, these will broadly cover the customers' characteristics – the descriptors which outline the individual and organisational characteristics of the customers and their context, the situation in which they are acquiring our products and services.

The customer profile does not have to be exhaustive, but it needs to give a specific picture of the nature of the customer group. This clarity is needed, first, in order to avoid any ambiguity about which particular groups the organisation is focusing on and, second, in order to enable us to explore the customer value and price dimensions which are outlined in the next stage. Any strategy is likely to require a number of these strategic customer profiles to be drawn up. For example, a customer acquisition strategy based on referral needs to identify both those who are likely to provide referrals, either actively or passively, and those who are likely to adopt your products and services based on these referrals. In all likelihood these two groups will have quite distinct customer profiles.

Having identified the direction of our customer strategy and the strategic customer profiles of the groups on which we need to focus, next we need to work out the position from which we are to compete for these customers' business. Here we use the customer matrix as a basis for doing this.

Strategic customer profile: Multiple retailer	
Characteristics	National coverage, own-brand development, high-value proposition (not discounted), high growth expectations
Context	Ongoing relationship, regular business transactions, contacts, relationship seen as important part of both our activities

Figure 5.6 Example of a strategic customer profile

THE POSITIONING OF CUSTOMER STRATEGIES –
THE CUSTOMER MATRIX

The customer matrix is a framework developed by Cliff Bowman at the Cranfield School of Management. Its power lies in its simple elegance and, most importantly, in the way it forces managers to ask fundamental questions about the way in which they are seen by their customers.

The customer matrix is shown in Figure 5.7. It has two axes. The vertical axis represents perceived use value, that is the value the customer derives from using or acquiring the product. The horizontal axis represents price, as perceived by the customer. These two dimensions provide a basis on which we can consider how customers see the various competitive offerings in the marketplace.

The key to using the customer matrix is to note that it is from the perspective of a customer. Indeed, it is meaningless to undertake this with some general sense of a particular market in mind – it needs to be done with a very clear idea of who the customer is and how they respond. Then, the strategic customer profile can be applied in order to introduce a perspective for analysis.

In terms of thinking about our customers, the customer matrix has three main functions. First, it forces us to identify the basis on which customers assess value. For example, if we are in the business of systems service support, our target customers may assess value in terms of the speed with which we respond to faults, the

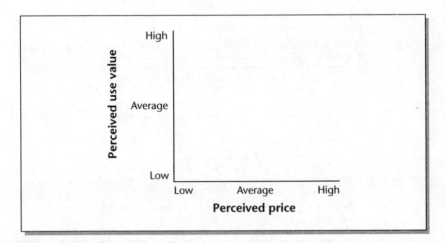

Figure 5.7 The customer matrix
Source: Bowman and Faulkner[1]

unconditional service guarantees we provide and the calibre of our staff. Whatever these dimensions may be, it is fundamental to our competitive strategy that we identify them and manage the way our actions are perceived by the customer.

The second benefit of the customer matrix is that it allows us to assess how we are positioned relative to our competitors in the eyes of customers. This can often be a salutary exercise, when it becomes evident that we are significantly below our competitors in terms of perceived value and yet we are charging a higher price than they are.

The third benefit is that it allows us to consider the direction in which we may want to move in order to secure a competitive advantage when dealing with this particular type of customer.

Identifying the dimensions of perceived use value

In order to use the customer matrix, we need to calibrate the vertical axis, perceived use value (PUV). Figure 5.8 illustrates how the value dimensions used by customers can be represented. Further examples are provided in Bowman and Faulkner.[1]

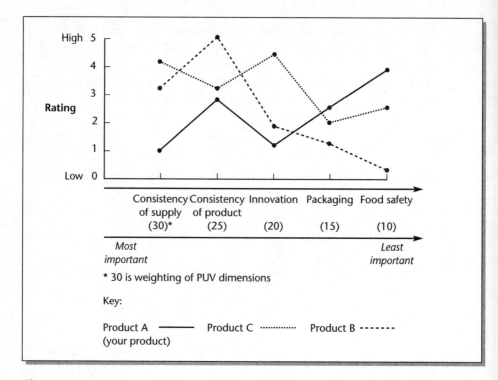

Figure 5.8 Dimensions of the perceived use value

In the case of the food manufacturer outlined earlier, the dimensions of the PUV for the retailer are consistency of supply, consistency of product, innovation, packaging and food safety. In addition to identifying the PUV dimensions, these are also weighted in order to establish which are the most important to customers. As can be seen from Figure 5.8, product A is performing particularly well on the dimensions which are of least value to the customer. The important point to note regarding the PUV dimensions is that they are specific to particular types of customers. If we were to redo the exercise for a food services customer, the dimensions would be more likely to look like those shown in Figure 5.9.

Figure 5.9 shows that the customer profile in the food services sector has similar PUVs, but that these have quite different relative weightings. In this case, the need for food handling by a food services company and the link between any outbreaks of food poisoning and their own reputation makes food safety a critical issue. This is therefore relatively more important to this group than it is to a multiple retailer. Similarly, the ability of the product to perform under varying conditions is far more important for this customer than for a retailer. All these factors are, of course, important to both, but there is a distinct difference in emphasis for these two customer profiles.

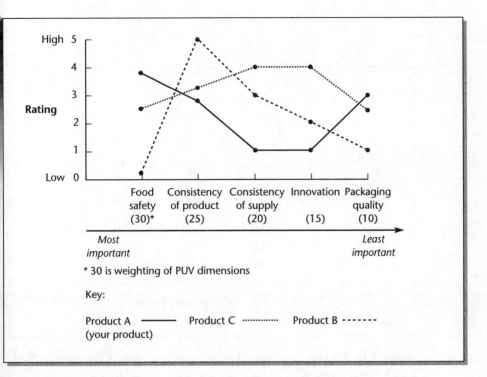

Figure 5.9 The PUV dimensions for a food services company

121

Competitive positioning from the customers' perspective

Having established the differences between the PUV dimensions, these can be combined with a price level to plot the competitive positioning as seen by customers. These are summarised in Table 5.1.

The co-ordinates outlined in Table 5.1 can now be plotted on the customer matrix, as shown in Figure 5.10.

Table 5.1 The customer matrix co-ordinates for a multiple retailer

PUV dimensions	Weight	Product A		Product B		Product C	
		Rating	Score	Rating	Score	Rating	Score
Consistency of supply	30	1	30	3	90	4	120
Consistency of product	25	3	75	5	125	3	75
Innovation	20	1	20	2	40	4.5	90
Packaging	15	2.5	37.5	1	15	2	30
Food safety	10	4	40	0.5	5	2.5	25
Total			202.5		275		340
Price			0.92		0.98		1.08

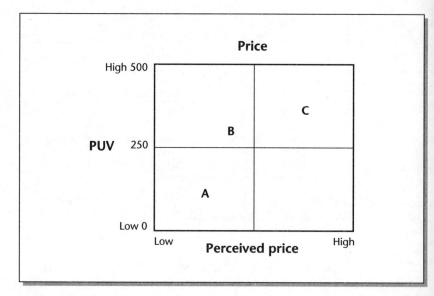

Figure 5.10 Plotting competitors on the customer matrix from the multiple retailer's perspective

From Figure 5.10, our company (A) is seen by the multiple retailer as being relatively lower in value and price terms than the two major competitors, B and C. This is a perfectly reasonable position to be in, as long as we have a lower cost base than our competitors.

In the case of a food services customer, the picture looks quite different, as we can see from Table 5.2 and Figure 5.11.

Table 5.2 The customer matrix co-ordinates for a food service business

PUV dimensions	Weight	Product A		Product B		Product C	
		Rating	Score	Rating	Score	Rating	Score
Food safety	30	4	120	0.5	15	2.5	75
Consistency of product	25	3	75	5	125	3	75
Consistency of supply	20	1	20	3	60	4	80
Innovation	15	1	15	2	30	4.5	67.5
Packaging	10	2.5	25	1	10	2	20
Total			255		240		317.5
Price			0.92		0.98		1.08

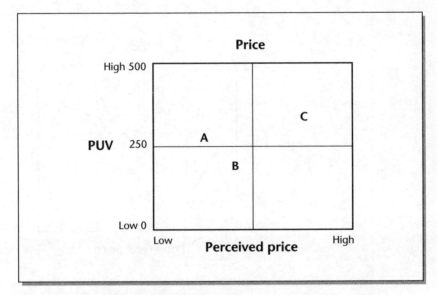

Figure 5.11 Plotting competitors on the customer matrix from the perspective of a food service business

When comparing Figure 5.10 with Figure 5.11, it can be seen that the the multiple retailer values the offering of company B over ours (company A), whereas when we consider the different offers from the point of view of a food services business, company A's offer is seen as having the greater value.

This raises a number of questions concerning the competitive strategy of company A. If, as is the case here, most of company A's business goes through multiple retailers, it needs to address its positioning in the market. However, it is well placed to serve food services organisations and, therefore, in the future, this could form an important source of revenue for the company.

Determining competitive options

A major benefit of the customer matrix is that it allows us to consider where we might move in order to achieve competitive advantage *in the eyes of customers*.

The value-for-money curve shown in Figure 5.12 represents the points at which there is an acceptable combination of perceived use value and price, which means that customers are happy to acquire products or services located on this average curve (Bowman and Faulkner[6]). If an organisation is able to offer superior value and a lower price to

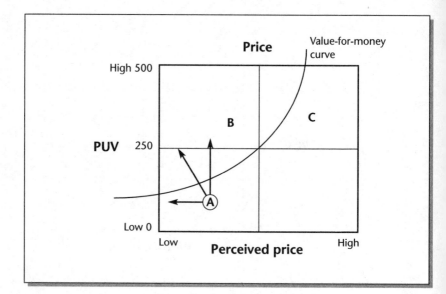

Figure 5.12 The value-for-money curve and alternative directions on the customers matrix from a multiple retailer's perspective

that depicted by the curve, then this organisation has a competitive advantage from the customers' viewpoint. We can see from Figure 5.12 that company B is in such a position, offering higher value at a lower price than the average value for money in the sector. This is primarily due to company B's high scores in delivering consistency of supply and consistency of product to the retailers.

When considering company A's potential moves, one option is moving north on the matrix in order to add more value at the same price. This could be achieved by improving performance with regard to supply and innovation or by cutting the price in order to offer the same value at present but at a significantly reduced price. In order to sustain a move west, company A would first have to establish whether or not this was sustainable in terms of its cost position in comparison with B and C.

In Figure 5.13, we see a distinctly different situation in terms of the potential options open to company A. It could enhance its profitability by increasing its prices. This would still keep its product within the value-for-money curve, although it could undermine its relationship with its customers and its significant advantage over the competition would be removed. By moving north, enhancing its value, it could work more closely with its customers to enhance value further, thereby developing a sustainable position over its competitors.

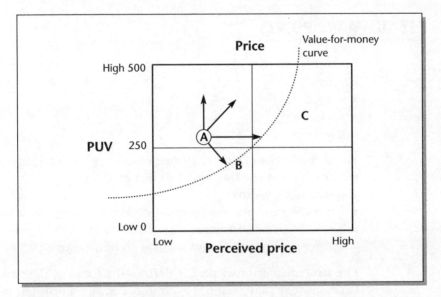

Figure 5.13 The value-for-money curve and alternative directions on the customer matrix as used by a food services organisation

The examples we have looked at to show how to go about applying the customer matrix to two distinct customer profiles underlines how competitive advantage is never absolute – it is relative and is created and supported by the particular customer profile we consider. In the case of company A, it has a choice in terms of the strategic direction (as opposed to minor tactical adjustments and cosmetic changes) the business could take. It should either focus on benchmarking against competitor B, focusing on multiple retailers and ensuring that it develops its logistics and manufacturing capability further, or else concentrate on the food services sector, using its technology in food safety to acquire further customers and build up its presence in this particular sector. This latter option it seems particularly well placed to do, although the cultural implications for a business that has grown and based its strategy on selling to retailers could present significant barriers to its implementation. These are discussed in more detail in Chapter 7.

A final point to note is that the customer matrix has been used here on the basis of the managers' judgements as to how its strategic customers see value and price. This is important as it raises questions about what we know and what perhaps we should know but do not. In either event, it is important that these issues are substantiated by research so we are clear as to the nature of the real dimensions used by these customers.

KEY SUMMARY POINTS

1 Customer strategies can be considered as having three key elements:
   - direction
   - focus
   - position.

2 The direction of customer strategy involves considering whether or not the business will be based on:
   - developing loyalty
   - extending the business generated with existing customers
   - acquiring new customers
   - selling new products and services to new customers.

3 The strategic customer profile defines the focus of the strategy. Each strategy may well have a number of these profiles, but it is important that they are clearly defined throughout the organisation.

4 The customer matrix is an approach to considering competitive positioning from the customers' point of view.

5 The customer matrix requires that we identify the basis on which customers assesses value and price.

6 Because different customer groups see price and value in different ways, we can find more advantagous positions by focusing on a different customer group.

7 This application of the customer matrix has been based on individuals making judgements about customers' views. It is important that these dimensions are validated with the customers themselves.

KEY QUESTIONS AND DIAGNOSTICS

Does your organisation have a clear view as to where it is going, who it is focusing on and its relative positioning with regard to customers?

Plot where you think your company is located on the customer growth matrix. Where do you think the future emphasis should be? What issues does this raise for the organisation?

Write down the three most important strategic customer groups for the organisation. Get some of your colleagues to do the same. Are they different? If so, why?

STRATEGIC THINKING DIAGNOSTIC

Score each of these statements in terms of how strongly you agree or disagree with them. Add up the scores and see what your total means.

	Agree			Disagree	
In our organisation, we just take any customer we can, whether they are repeat business or new business.	1	2	3	4	5
We do not differentiate between existing and new customers.	1	2	3	4	5
There is very little agreement as to which types of customers we should be focusing on.	1	2	3	4	5
We leave things like customer profiles to our advertising or research agencies.	1	2	3	4	5
We frequently work out exactly which customers should be the focus of our efforts.	5	4	3	2	1
We really have little idea about what customers really value in our product or service.	1	2	3	4	5
We gave never really considered whether some groups of customers value what we do more than others.	1	2	3	4	5

Score

25–35: You have a clear, focused customer strategy.

15–25: Some areas are OK, but there is room for improvement.

0–15: There is a lack of clarity and precision to the strategy of the organisation.

REFERENCES

1 As outlined in Bowman, C., and Faulkner, D. (1997), *Competitive and Corporate Strategy*, London, Irwin

2 Ansoff, H. I. (1965), *Corporate Strategy*, New York, McGraw-Hill

3 For example, Christopher, M., Payne, A., and Ballantyne, D. (1992), *Relationship Marketing*, Oxford, Butterworth–Heinemann, and Reichheld, F. F. (1996), *The Loyalty Effect*, Boston, MA, Harvard Business School Press

4 ibid.

5 Meldrum, N. (1992), Multi-electronique et CIE, Cranfield, Beds, Cranfield School of Management

6 ibid.

6

CHAPTER

MATCHING
CUSTOMERS TO
COMPETENCES

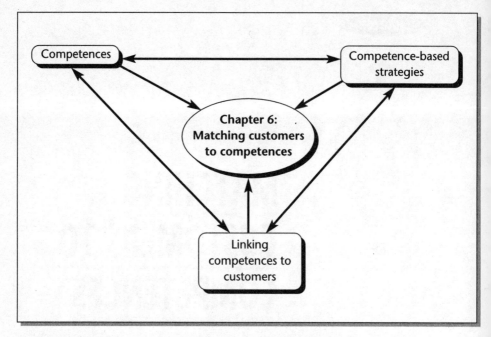

Figure 6.1 Overview map of the subjects covered in Chapter 6

So far, we have considered which customers we should regard as strategic and the various strategies we can use to develop our business with them. In the last chapter we also began to consider the issue of sustainable competitive advantage. In this chapter, we explore this issue further and, in particular, identify how it can be linked to the selection and development of strategic customers by linking customers with competences.

In Figure 6.1 we can see that the focus of this chapter is an exploration of the relationship between customers, represented by the strategic competence profile, and the competences of the organisation. The rationale for looking at these issues is that when unique organisational competences are matched to customer groups, sustainable competitive advantage is achieved.

The term 'sustainable competitive advantage' comes from the work of Michael Porter.[1] Porter refers to sustainable competitive advantage as being the generation of profits that are above the average for the industry which are sustained in the long run. Profit is therefore the outcome when an organisation achieves sustained competitive advantage. Organisations such as British Airways and Coca-Cola have attained returns significantly above the average for their industries for a period in excess of five years. The idea behind this book, as outlined in Chapter 1, is that above-average, long-run profitability can be achieved by defining and creating relationships with particular types of customers. A key element in this argument is that specific types of customers either see enhanced value in what such companies offer or provide a cost advantage to them or, ideally, can do both of these.

In order to explore how we can develop sustainable advantage, we now consider how to analyse three key elements of sustainable competitive advantage:

- competences
- rarity
- sustainability.

COMPETENCES

Competences are concerned with the capabilities of the organisation – what it is that the organisation is good at, as opposed to the skills or competencies of particular individuals. The term 'core competence' originates from the work of Prahalad and Hamel,[2] although many of the ideas and concepts behind it are drawn from the resource-based theory of the firm.[3] In essence, the notion of competences is the same as that of strengths and weaknesses in the ubiquitous SWOT analysis. The distinction is that finding core competences involves taking a far more detailed look at the capabilities of the organisation and their role in achieving sustained competitive advantage.

Competences are distinguished from resources in the organisation in that they consist of combinations of resources and are created as a result of the ways in which these resources are connected together. For example, Figure 6.2 shows a typical list of the sorts of resources we might come up with as part of a SWOT analysis.

While such resources are undoubtedly essential for the functioning of an organisation, they are less important for the development of sustainable competitive advantage because they are tradable and are therefore relatively easy for our competitors to acquire. The term 'competence' is normally associated with a higher-level capability, one concerned with the way in which resources are brought together.

In Figure 6.3, we can see that, while this organisation has a set of particular resources, the competence is created by connecting together a number of elements in a unique way. In this case, the knowledge, systems and cash combine to create an organisational competence in cash management. This is a competence whereas a large amount of cash or a sophisticated cash management system are discrete resources.

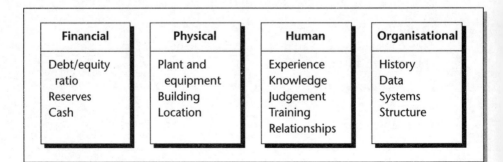

Financial	Physical	Human	Organisational
Debt/equity ratio	Plant and equipment	Experience	History
Reserves	Building	Knowledge	Data
Cash	Location	Judgement	Systems
		Training	Structure
		Relationships	

Figure 6.2 Examples of some organisational resources

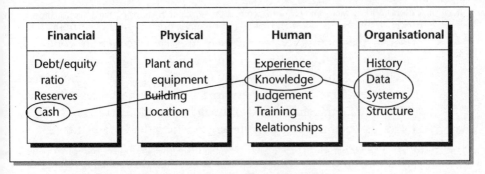

Figure 6.3 A competence arises from the linking of resources

In line with the concept of this book, we will now consider competences in terms of what is needed to serve particular customer groups. Note, though, that the emphasis of the resource-based theory of the firm is on internal introspection. However, this does not provide a basis for considering the relative aspects of competence. For example, if we have a competence in innovation, how does this generate value for our customers and who do we compare ourselves with in order to establish an advantage?

In order to evaluate competences we need to ask ourselves which competences are needed in order to create value in the eyes of our customers (what their PUVs are) or in order to reduce the cost of serving a particular customer (this provides flexibility within the price dimension of the customer matrix). It is therefore assumed that competences are only of value if they add to perceived use values for customers or if they allow us to serve customers for a lower cost than that of our competitors. In this context, competences are therefore never absolute – they are always relative to our customer profiles and relevant competitors.

RARITY

Having competences in things – such as innovation – is all well and good, but if they are held by all the major competitors because they are a fundamental part of being in this particular industry (say, pharmaceuticals), then it is a source of competitive *parity*, not competitive *advantage*.

One of the problems with the way in which the SWOT analysis is used is that it is not challenging or discriminating enough to determine the basis of competitive advantage. An analogy can be drawn here with Herzberg's 'two factor' theory.[4] In this theory of motivation, factors are defined as being either 'hygienic' – their presence does not motivate, but their absence or reduction would demotivate – or 'motivating' – their presence strongly motivates the individual. In this context, hygiene factors are the basic competences that are needed to be in business. In the case of pharmaceuticals one such would be the ability to continually develop new drugs. Motivating factors are the competences which deliver advantage, above the hygiene level. To continue our example, a competence of this kind would be getting products to market particularly quickly or cost-effectively.

It is fundamental that we are able to distinguish between the competences which deliver parity and are common to the industry and those which deliver advantage and are rare. In order to do this, we need a greater level of detail. For example, the 'ability to innovate' is a broad category which may include many elements, such as the ability to generate ideas, recruit and motivate creative staff, develop sophisticated reporting systems to ensure that ideas are effectively screened before moving on to more expensive evaluation stages and so on. All of these are part of the ability to innovate, but it may be in these sub-elements that the rare competence exists.

SUSTAINABILITY

In organisations, as in life in general, nothing can be said to be truly sustainable, but if it can be sustained for some time, it can be the basis of competitive advantage. If a competence can be quickly copied by the competition, then it fast loses its value as the competitive advantage it afforded could not be sustained and so is not of long-term benefit to the organisation.

Many organisations and consultants have visited the Disney Corporation in order to define the essence of the competences which have enabled Disney to become such an example of an organisation which has achieved sustained competitive advantage in the long term in many of its business interests. However, the notion that such an essence can be noted and replicated appears to be, at best, optimistic. The nature of sustainability is that the competences behind it are difficult to imitate. Often these competences are embedded in the organisation so they are difficult to recognise and to imitate. Such competences involve complicated interactions and relationships, such as dealing with customers. For example, Proctor & Gamble has made itself the preferred supplier to many of the large retail groups. This has been achieved by means of its ethos of building relationships with retailers in order to save each other costs and add value to consumers. The way in which the whole organisation works is to build linkages across functions, such as logistics, finance, marketing and operations, between suppliers and customers. This increases the contact areas between the organisations, making it increasingly difficult for competitors to make inroads and, therefore, building a *sustainable* competitive advantage.

COMPETENCES AND CUSTOMERS

In terms of the agenda for this book, the issue of competences as a basis for sustainable competitive advantage raises two fundamental points. The first concerns the link between competences and strategic customer profiles, summarised in Figure 6.4.

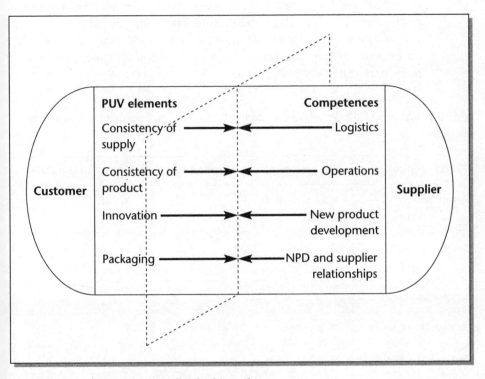

Figure 6.4 The customer–supplier looking glass

Figure 6.4 shows how the customer-driven parameters of perceived use values can be specifically linked to competences within the organisation. This linking process is particularly important as it provides synthesis between our understanding of our strategic customers and the competences of the organisation. If the type of customer is of strategic importance, then the links between them and our competences need to be explicit in order to ensure that the organisation is in fact delivering that which the customer values. I will use the short management courses of a fictitious business school as an example of this process.

A study of delegates on the courses showed the following three core PUV elements:

1 reputation
2 ability of the course to add to delegates' personal development
3 the course facilities.

Each of these elements related to an area of competence, as summarised in Table 6.1.

The first stage in this process is to translate how a particular PUV dimension will translate into a competence. From Table 6.1 it can be seen that the PUV dimension of 'course facilities' is matched with the competence of a four-star hotel culture. There may be other competences which are relevant, but we need to identify those which we believe have the most impact with the customers concerned in influencing the PUV dimension.

Table 6.1 Matching PUV dimensions to competences, for management development delegates

PUV dimensions	Competences	Competence	Rarity	Sustainability
Reputation	Track record Media relations	1 2	1 1	1 1
My development	Visible frameworks Course design	2 2	1 1	1 1
Course facilities	4-star hotel culture	2	1	1
Competence score	**90 per cent**	9	5	5
Sustained advantage score	**50 per cent**			

Table 6.1 also includes a figure for how well the organisation feels it scores in terms of achieving a sustainable competitive advantage. Competence is therefore not treated as a categorical or nominal variable – you either have it or you do not – but as an ordinal variable – which means you rate your level of competence relative to the competition. In the case of competence, the scale for the scores is as follows:

- 0 = no competence;
- 1 = some competence;
- 2 = outstanding.

It can be seen from Table 6.1 that this business school has a very high level of competence in meeting the needs of this particular group. Using these scales, the competence rating from this customer group is 9, from a potential maximum of 10. The competence score for this customer group is therefore 90 per cent.

However, the level of competence only provides us with part of the picture. We also need to evaluate how rare these particular types of competence are and whether or not they are sustainable. In order to do this, we are not using our organisation as the focus for analysis, but the competences which we have identified. In other words, we are considering whether or not this competence is generally rare, and whether or not it would be difficult to imitate or copy over time, regardless of who may develop this competence.

Rarity can be scored using the following descriptors:

0 = common to all;
1 = limited to a small group of suppliers;
2 = unique to one particular supplier.

Sustainability is scored as follows:

0 = can be copied or substituted very quickly;
1 = some copying is possible, but needs time to reach the same level;
2 = virtually impossible to replicate in the medium term.

The scores for rarity and sustainability are combined in an overall score of sustained advantage. In the case of our example, this score is less positive, the overall value being 50 per cent. This indicates that, while the organisation is performing well in serving this customer group, so are the major competitors, and most of the competences needed are difficult to sustain in the long run.

In contrast, Table 6.2 shows the competence profile for another customer group. In this case, it is for a pan-European MBA programme with a mixture of students from most of the member states of the EU. The UK MBA market is relatively mature and oversupplied, so the business school is considering the possibility of a customer acquisition strategy to develop a truly pan-European MBA. It would like to acquire more non-UK students from continental Europe.

The PUV dimension 'reputation' is believed to be created by a strong European alumni body. As a result of frequent exposure in the continental business media, media relations is a competence, and, similarly, as staff have had articles and so on published in pan-European journals and books, European publications is a competence.

As can be seen from the analysis presented in Table 6.2, this organisation does not perform particularly well on these competences (the competence score is 30 per cent). However the analysis also indicates that no one else possesses these competences and that, if competence is developed in these areas, it would be relatively unique and so it would be difficult for competitors to imitate it (creating a sustained advantage score of 95 per cent). So, while there is an apparent opportunity for achieving a sustainable advantage, this is far removed from the competence base of this organisation. Thus, such a strategy may be unrealistic or extremely costly to implement, but it may be possible to obtain these competences by means of an alliance or joint venture with other European business schools.

Table 6.2 Matching PUV dimensions to competences, for continental MBA students

PUV dimensions	Competences	Competence	Rarity	Sustainability
Reputation	European alumni	0	2	2
	European media	0	2	2
	European publications	1	2	1
Quality of students	Age of students	1	2	2
	Experience of students	1	2	2
Competence score	**30 per cent**			
Sustained advantage score	**95 per cent**			

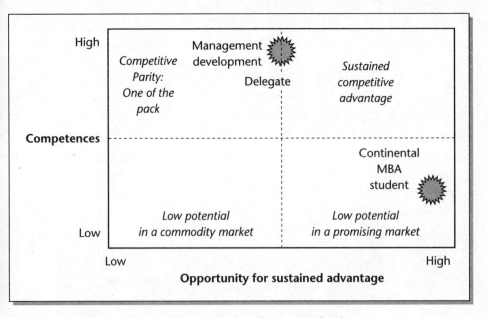

Figure 6.5 Customer competence matrix for a business school

The results of the assessments of the two strategic customer groups shown in Tables 6.1 and 6.2 can be plotted on a chart, as shown in Figure 6.5. Figure 6.5 shows the positioning of these two customer groups for the business school. If *all* strategic customer profiles are plotted in this way, the result is an overview of the relative positioning of the different groups in terms of achieving a sustainable competitive advantage.

Having plotted where the customers fall on the chart, it is then possible to determine where the most effective route to achieving sustained competitive advantage can be found. Figure 6.6 illustrates the two basic routes.

First, by moving northwards, the organisation is developing the competences needed to create value for this particular customer group. In the case of the business school, this could be by recruiting more pan-European staff with records of having work published in other European countries, building the capability to set up multiple exchanges with other European business schools and a resource to develop pan-European, multilingual teaching materials. All of these options will require significant investment, both in terms of managerial commitment and financial resources. The trade-off that has to be weighed up is whether or not such investment will provide the benefits once these competences have been created.

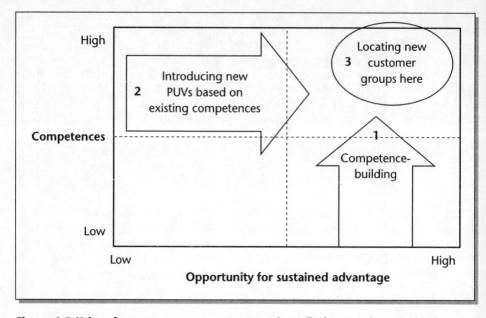

Figure 6.6 Using the customer competence matrix to find routes for sustained competitive advantage

The second option is to move east. This is more problematical, but considerable benefits can be reaped as the organisation is building on existing competences and is therefore well placed to develop a strong position. In this second option, new elements of PUV are developed which match the organisation's existing competence. The challenge is to be able to change customer perceptions in order to establish a new dimension of PUV. For example, travel agents are a strategic customer group for airlines as many travellers rely on the agent to select the most appropriate carrier for when and where they wish to travel. Traditionally it has been difficult for airlines to build any form of sustained advantage with travel agents. However, with the development of on-line booking systems, which allow the travel agent to make a booking directly onto the airline's system, using these systems makes the operation faster and easier for the agent. This has meant that systems such as Galileo (British Airways and partners' system) and Sabre (American Airlines and partners' system) has allowed airlines with high IT competence to develop sustainable competitive advantage in their relationships with travel agents.

Michael Eisner is attributed with turning round the Disney Corporation,[5] not because he came up with some novel strategy, but because he concentrated on the competences which Disney already had, such as launching some of the Disney classics on video and regenerating the making of feature-length cartoons. In this case, the competences already existed – it was just a question of getting more from these competences in order to build sustained advantage.

In the case of the example of the business school, it may be that this particular organisation has a competence in a particular aspect of running an MBA programme, such as experiential learning. Because this is a relatively rare competence, it offers the school significant potential to create a sustained competitive advantage if the business school also has the competence to communicate this to the market in a way which augments the usual PUV dimensions potential students are using.

The third approach illustrated in Figure 6.6 is that if no customer groups fit into the sustained competitive advantage quadrant, then ask whether there are any new customers who would. For example, Dr Marten is an English boot and shoe manufacturer that uses a patented air-cushioned sole. Traditionally the company's products were sold as working boots, bought by organisations such as the police, where wearers were spending a lot of time on their feet and needed comfort and protection. However, the working footwear market was highly competitive and presented little opportunity for developing a sustained competitive advantage. By chance, the boots started to develop cachet as an alternative fashion accessory, particularly with teenagers and students. In this more fashionable market, there was more scope to make the most of the Dr Marten competences of well-made, comfortable footwear that had a very distinctive, rugged look. Hence, a new customer group was developed which enabled a struggling shoe company to develop into a well-known and highly profitable fashion business.

The issue for the third approach outlined in Figure 6.6 is to identify what we believe we have real competences in doing which are likely to be both rare and difficult to imitate, translate these into potential value dimensions and look for customers who may regard these as particularly important. This process is outlined in Figure 6.7.

It can be seen from Figure 6.7 that the competences found tend to be very specific and therefore suggest particular customer groups relatively easily. A vague description of a competence does not help produce the clarity needed to focus on particular customer groups.

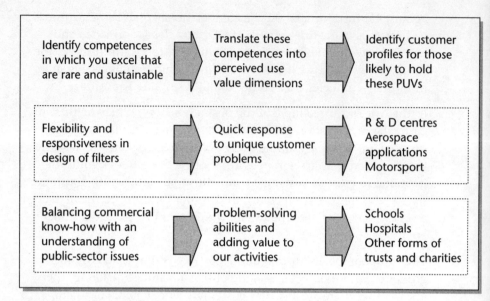

Figure 6.7 Using competences to find target customers

KEY SUMMARY POINTS

1 Sustainable competitive advantage can be achieved by matching unique organisational competences to specific customer profiles.

2 The three elements of sustained competitive advantage are:
   • competences,
   • rarity,
   • sustainability.

3 Competences are created by connecting combinations of resources in a unique way.

4 Competences are not absolute, but, rather, are relative to the customer profile being considered and the relevant group of competitors.

5 It is important to be able to differentiate between the competences which deliver parity and are common to the industry and those which deliver an advantage and are rare.

6 By establishing the competences needed to deliver PUV among those in our customer groups and the rarity and sustainability of the competences, we can identify those groups of customer where we can achieve a sustained competitive advantage.

7 Identifying the competences which are rare and sustainable can suggest further PUVs and customers the organisation can pursue.

KEY QUESTIONS AND DIAGNOSTICS

What are the competences of the organisation? Which of these are you particularly effective at and which are rare and sustainable?

Identify the PUV dimensions of your strategic customer profiles. Identify which competences are needed to deliver the different elements of the PUVs.

Ignoring the external world temporarily, write down the three fundamental competences which you believe the organisation possesses. Who are the customers who would particularly value these competences. Aim to identify at least three customer groups you do not serve at present.

STRATEGIC THINKING DIAGNOSTIC

Score each of these statements in terms of how strongly you agree or disagree with them. Add up the scores and see what your total means.

	Agree			Disagree	
There is a lack of clarity as to exactly which competences we really need to focus on.	1	2	3	4	5
We know our customers, but we do not really have a view on which competences are appropriate to which customers.	1	2	3	4	5
Nothing we do is rare or unique – we are just one of the pack.	1	2	3	4	5
We have no idea how good or bad we are in relation to the competition.	1	2	3	4	5
We regularly focus on competence-building initiatives.	5	4	3	2	1
We never really think seriously about what other groups of customers would value what we do.	1	2	3	4	5
We have never considered the possibility of adding to the way the customers see our products and services.	1	2	3	4	5

Score

25–35: Excellent awareness of competences and their relationship with customer value.

15–25: In the middle – perhaps there is the need to spend more time reflecting on the real competences of the organisation.

0–15: A concerning lack of focus on organisational competences.

SUGGESTED FURTHER READING

The following provide further insights into the notion of competences and their links with customers.

Barney, J. B. (1995), 'Looking Inside for Competitive Advantage', *Academy of Management Executive*, 9, 4, 49–61

Day, G. S. (1994), 'The Capabilities of Market-driven Organizations', *Journal of Marketing*. 58 (October), 37–52

Hamel, G., and Prahalad, C. K. (1994), *Competing for the Future*, Boston, MA, Harvard Business School Press

REFERENCES

[1] Porter, M. (1980), *Competitive Strategy*, New York, Free Press, and Porter, M. (1985), *Competitive Advantage*, New York, Free Press

[2] Prahalad, C. K., and Hamel, G. (1990), 'The Core Competence of the Corporation', *Harvard Business Review*, May–June, 79–91

[3] For example, Barney, J. (1991), 'Firm Resources and Sustained Competitive Advantage', *Journal of Management*, **17**,1, 99–120, and Wernerfeldt, B. (1984), 'A Resource-based View of the Firm', *Strategic Management Journal*, **5**, 171–80

[4] Herzberg, F., Mausner, B, and Snyderman, B. (1959), *The Motivation to Work*, New York, Wiley

[5] See Grant, R. M. (1995), *Contemporary Strategy Analysis*, Cambridge, MA, Blackwell

CHAPTER 7

MAKING IT ALL HAPPEN – THE CUSTOMER-FOCUSED ORGANISATION

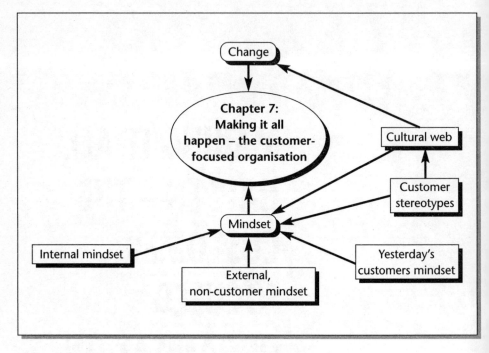

Figure 7.1 Overview map of the topics covered in Chapter 7

Up to this point we have been concerned with *intended* strategies. We have been working through a process which is intended to enhance the performance of the organisation by developing a strategic focus on customer profiles. However, we have not, so far, considered many of the organisational issues which may inhibit or advance the adoption of a customer-oriented approach to strategy.

The purpose of this chapter is to reflect on the organisational issues which may influence the realisation of a customer-focused strategy and, in particular, the incorporation of customer-driven thinking into the strategy processes of the organisation. Figure 7.1 provides an overview map for this chapter.

As can be seen from Figure 7.1, this chapter is constructed around a discussion on organisational mindsets as a basis for evaluating the ability of the organisation to deliver a customer-focused strategy. Supporting the notion of organisational mindsets are the culture of organisations, which we will explore using Gerry Johnson's cultural web,[1] and, from this, the issues raised concerning organisational change.

While there are many excellent books on organisational change and culture,[2] few have really dwelt on the issue of how customers may be brought into and sustained in the minds of those working in organisations.[3] Here, we consider a number of differing levels at which thinking strategically about customers may occur in the organisations. In order to develop these ideas we first need to establish the principle of organisational mindsets.

MINDSETS

The word 'mindset' is a term used for shared beliefs and assumptions. Research has indicated that such mindsets may operate at different levels. For example, Spender[4] talks of 'industry recipes', by which is meant that there is an accepted view as to how you do things in a particular industry. This has been reinforced by other studies, such as a review of the US domestic airline industry,[5] which indicated that most of the organisations followed similar types of strategy. Where radical change occurs in an industry, it is where a player breaks the mindset, such as Dell's move to sell PCs direct to customers in the

1980s rather than using the traditional network. Daewoo cars have been particularly successful in the UK market by developing a different way of selling cars using sales centres where non-commissioned advisers offer advice on different models. There is even a crèche where children can play while their parents consider the different products on offer. These companies have broken the traditional models of how you compete in their industries.

Mindsets also operate at the organisational level. Prahalad and Bettis[6] refer to this as the 'dominant logic' – the set of assumptions and values which pervade the organisation and which are influential both in its strategy formulation process (when it rejects options which do not fit with the dominant logic) and, perhaps more importantly, its strategy implementation, influencing how people actually behave in the organisation. It is also logical to assume that mindsets will also operate at functional levels. A marketing department, for example, may have a particular mindset which assumes that no major decision must be made without lengthy market research, that no new product can be launched without an expensive advertising campaign and so on.

At these various levels, mindsets influence the basis on which information is perceived or interpreted, the way it is stored in the memory and the way in which we behave as individuals. Mindsets are therefore fundamental to the functioning, and ultimately the performance, of the organisation. The organisational mindset is a double-edged sword. It may, in fact, provide the basis for sustained competitive advantage if it is in alignment with the environment because a mindset is idiosyncratic and therefore rare and as it is created by the cultural fabric of the organisation over time, it is also highly sustainable. However, if it does *not* align with the environment, it can cause the company to be highly dysfunctional and, because it is embedded in the way the organisation operates, it is also particularly difficult to change. Thus, it can also be the basis for sustained competitive *disadvantage*.

Figure 7.2 shows four potential mindset levels which are relevant in terms of thinking strategically about customers. Next, we shall explore some of the characteristics and implications of these.

An internal mindset

At this level, the customers do not feature in the dominant mindset of the organisation. This is a central concern for those who advocate the establishment of a marketing orientation.[7] A marketing

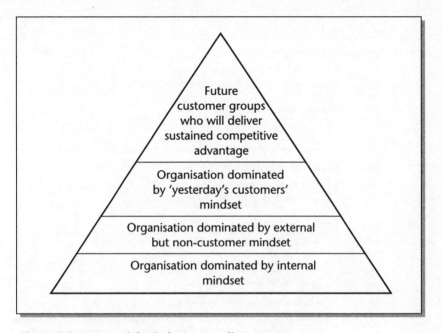

Figure 7.2 Managerial mindsets regarding customers

orientation has been described as that which is created by a number of key elements, which include a competitor orientation and interfunctional co-ordination.[8] However, in an in-depth study of practising managers, a group of American academics concluded that the dominant aspect of a marketing orientation is a clear and overriding focus on customers.[9]

As a way of clarifying the nature of customer orientation, it can be helpful to consider what the alternative orientations may be. Other orientations have been described as the product orientation, where the focus is on creating products, the capacity orientation, which is concerned with optimising plant, the technology orientation, which is concerned with the continual drive for new and more complicated technology, and the sales orientation, which is concerned with making products and then selling them as hard as possible. Some of the more widely accepted non-customer orientations are summarised in Figure 7.3.

All of these mindsets are characterised by their focus inwards. They are concerned with what we are most familiar with, the internal workings of the organisation, not what is going on 'out there' in the external environment.

153

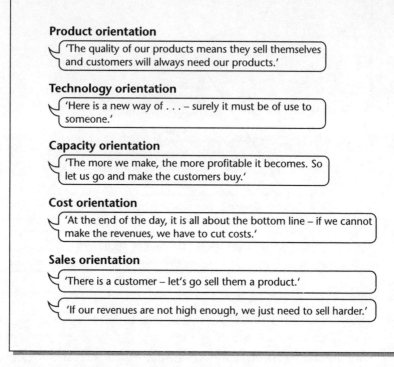

Product orientation

'The quality of our products means they sell themselves and customers will always need our products.'

Technology orientation

'Here is a new way of . . . – surely it must be of use to someone.'

Capacity orientation

'The more we make, the more profitable it becomes. So let us go and make the customers buy.'

Cost orientation

'At the end of the day, it is all about the bottom line – if we cannot make the revenues, we have to cut costs.'

Sales orientation

'There is a customer – let's go sell them a product.'

'If our revenues are not high enough, we just need to sell harder.'

Figure 7.3 Examples of internal mindsets

An external, non-customer mindset

There are other mindsets which are considered to be customer-facing, but in reality are not. These include brand orientation, where the company philosophy is about brand creation and development, the brand manager reigns supreme and the customer is relegated to being delivered to via rather complicated demographic market research. In this case, most of the emphasis and activity is being placed on relationships with advertising agencies and other forms of high-profile promotion activity.

Another such mindset is market orientation (as opposed to the marketing orientation), where there is a clear focus on a market, but not customers. Emphasis is placed on market share measures and market trend extrapolations. We sell into a market and are market-facing, but we do not discriminate between the types of customers we focus on.

In a study of the perspectives which managers have of their outward world, Day and Nedungadi[10] drew a distinction between a customer orientation and a competitive orientation. In the case of competitive orientation, the focus of activity is the monitoring of competitive actions and responding to them. While this is fundamentally important, it cannot be seen as an end in its own right. It is how customers interpret these behaviours which has to be the strategic focus of the organisation or else they will be outcompeting their rivals at a game which has little relevance to customers and their values.

A 'yesterday's customers' mindset

The next level in Figure 7.2 is that of a customer mindset which focuses on yesterday's customers rather than on the customer groups which are needed for both today and tomorrow.

In order to explore this phenomenon we will use the concept of the 'customer stereotype'. The impact of the customer stereotype is summarised in Figure 7.4. Here a strategic review has identified a particular customer profile as being central to the future strategy of the business. However, this strategy has not been realised as the dominant mindset evokes a different customer stereotype which arises from those customers who have been important to the growth of the business in the past. The behaviours of those in the company are therefore being driven not by the new, intended strategy but by the inertia of the customer stereotype.

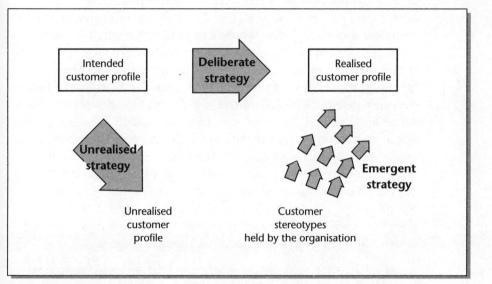

Figure 7.4 Distinguishing between intended and realised customer strategies
Source: Based on Mintzberg and Waters[11]

Customer stereotypes

A stereotype is a way of representing a particular group. It allows us to develop a model for anticipating the behaviour of other individuals or groups. Much of the literature on stereotypes has been from a negative perspective, considering the problems of racial and gender stereotyping, for example. However, more recently, social scientists have viewed this as a natural process which is fundamental for clarifying both individual and group identity, one which we apply to develop understanding and to decide how to act in differing situations.[12] Here we are concerned with using stereotyping as a way of bringing customers into our strategic thinking.

Research into this area has focused on stereotypes being described by a series of traits. In Katz and Brady's seminal study,[13] a list of traits was generated which students were then asked to assign to particular racial and cultural groups. The stereotype then became the top 12 traits listed by each group of 100 students. For example, Germans were described as scientifically minded, industrious and stolid, while Italians were described as artistic, impulsive, passionate, quick-tempered, the British as sportsmanlike, intelligent, conventional, tradition-loving, and Americans were considered industrious, intelligent, materialistic and ambitious.

More recently, researchers have used the relatively more complicated bipolar scale to ascertain stereotypes. In a study of sex role stereotypes,[14] a bipolar scale was used to describe the degree to which men or women were likely to have a particular characteristic. Such scales can be used to identify the types of traits which are used for stereotyping customers. If you use the trait approach, you simply identify the traits of your stereotype. For example, these may be that a customer stereotype is conservative, fair, adopts formal procedures and values long-term relationships. It is important to only include the traits which are considered relevant to the way in which your customers buy or use your product or service. The fact that a customer is a publicly quoted company or not is not necessarily relevant, but the fact that it buys in a very decentralised way would be. The bipolar scale presents the stereotype as points on a series of constructs. Figure 7.5 shows the scale which we have developed to capture some of the most common dimensions used by managers to think about customers.

In Figure 7.5 we also show the scores provided by senior managers from two banks, both in countries which were formerly part of the Soviet Union. Both respondents have applied the stereotype instrument to their commercial customers, which tend to use a range of facilities with them. As can be seen from the stereotype indicator, their scores are significantly different. The manager from the bank in Belarus describes his customer group as predominantly large, rigid, old and reactive. In contrast, the manager from the Estonian bank describes his customer stereotype as demanding, successful, innovative and young.

As mentioned, bipolar scales used in Figure 7.5 use some generic dimensions which have been found to apply across most organisations. In order to get real clarity, though, it is likely that dimensions specific to your customers also need to be entered in order to gain a detailed picture. For example, in the market map shown in Figure 4.3, the generic dimensions of rigid to flexible and specialist to generalist could be applied to the national distributors, but there are others, such as centralised purchasing, use of computerised logistics systems, which would add greater detail to the stereotype.

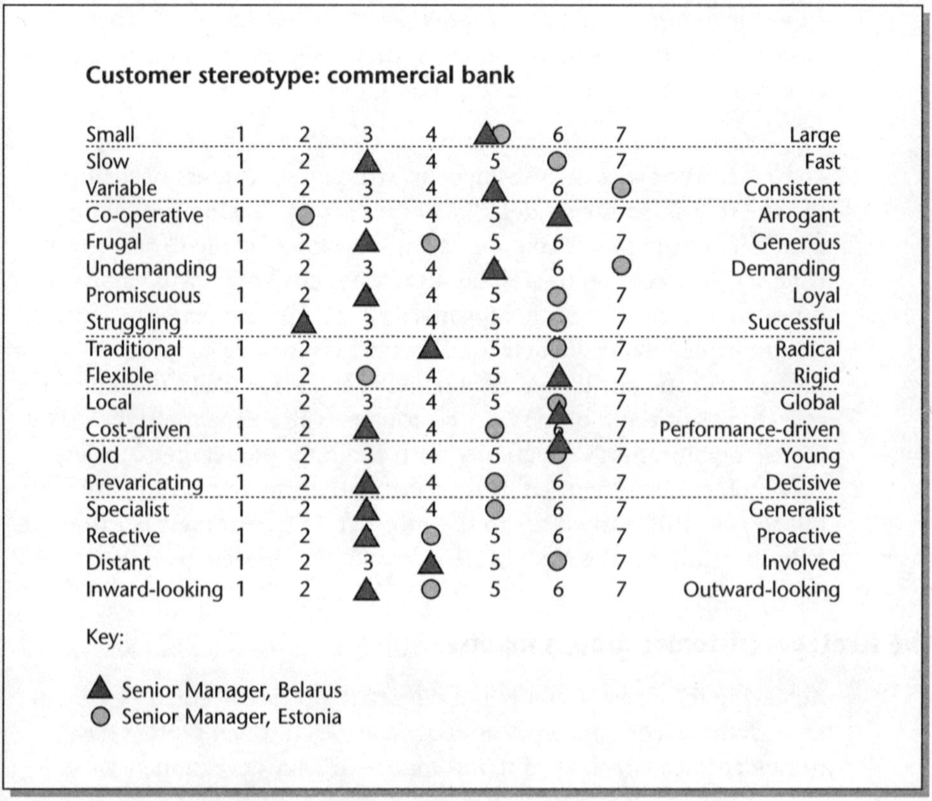

Customer stereotype: commercial bank

	1	2	3	4	5	6	7	
Small					▲◐			Large
Slow			▲			◯		Fast
Variable					▲		◯	Consistent
Co-operative		◯				▲		Arrogant
Frugal			▲	◯				Generous
Undemanding					▲	◯		Demanding
Promiscuous			▲			◯		Loyal
Struggling		▲				◯		Successful
Traditional				▲		◯		Radical
Flexible			◯			▲		Rigid
Local						◯▲		Global
Cost-driven			▲		◯	▲		Performance-driven
Old						◯▲		Young
Prevaricating			▲		◯			Decisive
Specialist			▲		◯			Generalist
Reactive			▲	◯				Proactive
Distant				▲	◯			Involved
Inward-looking			▲	◯				Outward-looking

Key:

▲ Senior Manager, Belarus
◯ Senior Manager, Estonia

Figure 7.5 Customer stereotypes represented on a bipolar scale

This illustrates the value of the stereotype as an analysis technique. First, it forces you to think in some detail about the types of customers you are serving and provides a picture for you to consider in your strategic analysis. This relates to the strategic customer profile outlined in Chapter 5. Second, it surfaces different preconceptions within the management team about the nature of customers and their relationships with you. This may, in fact, highlight that those concerned with formulating the strategy of the organisation may have radically different views about the identity and nature of customer groups and their value to the business. These are, of course, managers' individual perceptions, but the way we act is by means of our interpretations which are based on our perceptions. If we have a better understanding of these perceptions, then we can validate them – perhaps by means of external research – and we can compare them to check whether or not there is consensus or divergence about the nature of our customers. Divergence can, in fact, be very positive to the strategy development process as it can ensure that people continue to be challenged and prevent the discussion from degenerating into soporific group-think, but it is only positive if we know it is there. The advantage of the stereotype, then, is that it surfaces and makes explicit assumptions about strategic customer groups.

These factors are particularly important where there has been a change in the types of customers on which the business needs to focus – that is, in the strategic customer profile. Taking the food company outlined in Table 4.2, if the decision is made to switch to the food services companies, because these customers will value the unique competences of this organisation to a greater extent than will the multiple retailers which have formed the strategic customer profile over the last ten years of activity, then it is likely that the stereotypes of the food services customers will, in the main, be driven by the organisation's experience with the multiple retailers. Unless this problem is recognised, it is probable that the food company will fail to get sufficiently close to the food services customers because it is still operating on the basis of its stereotypes of yesterdays' customers.

The strategic customer groups mindset

Achieving this level of mindset implies that, on careful consideration of the external environment, a series of strategic customer profiles have been identified which need to inform the strategy development of the organisation. If such a strategy is to become reality, then it is necessary for these strategic customer profiles to be part of the shared assumptions and expectations of the business, for them to become part of the organisational mindset. This is the objective if the notion of the 'right type of customer' drives the hearts and minds of those developing and delivering the strategy of the organisation (that is, everyone).

The position we have sought to take in this book is a contingent one. There is no one right answer, in the sense that each organisation and its context are different and, therefore, to prescribe answers is misleading and simplistic. However, there is a need to ask better questions, and the outcome of such questions is the development of a more effective balance between the organisation and a focus on those customer groups which will enhance its long-term well-being.

The apex of the triangle in Figure 7.2 illustrates the achievement of such a balance, where advantage can be achieved by balancing mindset and competences with those customer groups which will be most beneficial to the development of the organisation. In order to achieve such a balance, the mindset of the organisation may need to change radically. An appreciation of the cultural fabric of the organisation is needed in order to conceive and implement effective change.

ORGANISATIONAL CULTURE

The 'culture' of an organisation can be seen as the fabric which supports and protects the mindset. One of the challenges in considering culture is to find ways in which the elements of the culture can be surfaced. One way in which we can consider the culture of an organisation is the 'cultural web', developed by Gerry Johnson.[15] This is summarised in Figure 7.6.

The cultural web consists of six elements which bind together to support the mindset of the organisation.[16] Johnson's position is that we can only really understand the nature of the mindset if we understand the six elements of the web. Similarly, we can only begin to change the mindset if we manage the elements which support and sustain it. The six elements of the web are:

- power
- organisational structure
- measures and controls
- rituals and routines
- myths and stories
- symbols.

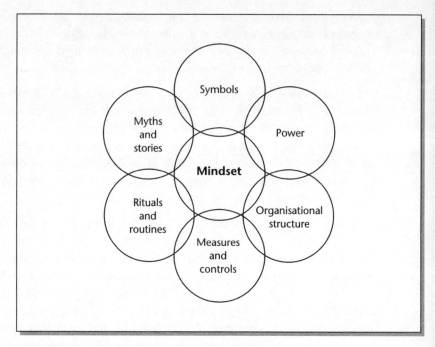

Figure 7.6 The cultural web of an organisation
Source: Johnson[15]

Power

'Power', in this context, means the individuals who are dominant in the decision making of the organisation, those who can act as a blockage or catalyst for change depending on whether or not they see this as being in their best interests. In a case study of an international airline,[17] the role of territory managers in dictating the marketing effort being put into various routes is discussed. In this case, the territory managers, while not the most senior in terms of the organisational chart, wielded most power in the organisation. Their view of customers is therefore more likely to dominate the implementation of strategy in the organisation than are the views of others.

Power may be supported by professional qualifications and reputation. For example, the head of an accountancy practice will be a chartered accountant, even though the position does not require the application of these professional skills. In many universities the dean or vice-chancellor will hold a Ph.D. and, again, this will not be required in the day-to-day work involved in this position, but it emphasises a particular power base in the organisation. It may also be that certain committees and project groups wield a great deal of power in an organisation, making membership of them much sought after. Power can be conferred, too – in terms of decision-making responsibility, but also in terms of implementation. Thus, particular groups may be powerful because it is up to them whether or not changes are actually implemented. Examples of powerful groups in organisations could be the consultants in a hospital, the administrators in a university, the buyers in a retail business and the salespeople in an industrial services business.

Let us look at an example of how such power can work. In one global organisation, a key dimension of its competitive advantage was believed to be the global nature of its business, which was in contrast to most of its competitors, which operated at a national or regional level. However, in delivering a pan-European strategy, the organisation experienced significant problems because of the power of the country managers. The country managers held the budgets and, as general managers, were all on the general management committee which developed and agreed strategy. As one individual succinctly put it, 'Getting the country managers to vote for a truly pan-European strategy is like getting turkeys to vote for Christmas'.

Organisational structure

Differing types of organisational structure reflect different cultures. For example, in retailing, most management activities are devolved to store level, with very few general management activities at the top. Alternatively the structure may be hierarchical, with clear reporting lines, which would probably be the case in government departments or organisations which were formerly state owned, such as the telecommunications or postal services.

A question to be considered here is does the formal structure dominate what happens or is there an informal network which is more influential in the running of the organisation? Also, is it who you know or who you report to which matters? This relates back to the issue of power. Structures may be simple or complicated, involving a multitude of linkages, making direct lines of responsibility very unclear. A functional structure, which emphasises particular areas of expertise, creates a different type of culture to that which is driven by customers and markets, mixing together different disciplines, such as operations, marketing and finance.

Measures and controls

These relate to the key measures which determine performance and define the achievements of groups and individuals. For example, measures which are based on market share will encourage a particular type of mindset which focuses on finding any way of increasing share, such as pulling orders forward or entering into price wars with competitors. For example, a large telecommunications organisation in the USA had spent huge amounts on developing a customer culture. However, at a training seminar the overriding topic of conversation over lunch was how the salespeople had achieved their targets for orders – no mention of customers at all. It is important that an organisation has measures and controls, but it also needs to be understood that these can have a significant impact on the actions and priorities of the individuals within the organisation and they should not be allowed to take over.

In retailing, the emphasis has shifted from gross margin to 'direct product profitability' (DPP). This has meant that lines which provided large margins have been dropped because they take up a great deal of space and the turnover for such stock is relatively slow. This shift in measures created a mindset change in both buyers and sellers. New opportunities were created for adding value because the DPP measure brought issues such as logistics performance and pack size to the forefront of the buyers' thinking.

In the consultancy business, utilisation of time – in the form of days which can be billed to clients – is a central performance criteria. Senior partners with heavy managerial responsibilities are therefore still making sure that they perform well on these measures, both in order to emphasise their own contribution to the business and to set an example to the junior consultants. This can cause the business to become dysfunctional if its overall strategy is to add value by extending the types of products and services which they sell to their clients.

In many organisations, managerial capability is assessed not on the potential to add customer value, but on the ability to cut costs. Measures such as performance versus budget create very clear priorities in terms of whether activities are investing in customer relationships for the future or cutting costs now.

Rituals and routines

These concern the activities which individuals engage in on a day-to-day basis. Routines are particularly powerful as they represent behaviours which are often the visible manifestation of the underlying mindset. For example, in a major consultancy practice, everything which was to be presented to the client had to be signed off by a partner beforehand, including letters and reports.[18] Routines may also be based on the hours people work, whether this be long hours in or out of the office or the partner coming in late or leaving early because of the habitual round of golf.

However, even strategic activity can become routinised. For example, as we have seen in the synthetic textile business, the development of the business has traditionally been built on a new fibre or process which can be protected by patent. The priorities of the business have come to be based on this routine, which means that other alternative approaches are never considered seriously. These strategies are embedded in the culture of the organisation.

Rituals are events such as rights of passage. These can be reflected in appraisal systems. For example, training programmes sometimes become ritualistic when being selected to go on the programme is seen as a sign of impending promotion. Activities such as dressing down on Fridays, Christmas parties and even regular meetings can become ritualistic when the behaviours are simply reinforcing the culture of the organisation. Planning processes can become important rituals, particularly in the relationships between business units and the corporate centre. Then, the planning process may be a ritual of getting the numbers to look right, so it is an activity which has little bearing on the behaviour of the business unit, but it keeps the corporate people off their backs and therefore it is a necessary ritual.

Myths and stories

Stories and myths are often about individuals – heroes, villains and mavericks. Maverick stories are often valuable in that they indicate what the mindset of the organisation is, based on considering the negative of this – what the mindset is not. In the case of the maverick, the story may be about the bank employee who ran up personal debts, the engineer who came to work at a conservative manufacturing company wearing a mohair jumper, ski-pants and winkle pickers.

Other stories are told about groups within the organisation – sales departments telling stories about those in production, finance telling stories about sales and so on – these stories being used to reflect differences, perhaps differences in skills and also differences in stature, of the various groups within the organisation.

Stories and myths also often relate to the founder of the organisation and his or her behaviours. For example, Massey Ferguson is one of the most well-known brands of agricultural machinery in the world. The organisation is still, even today, imbued with stories about Harry Ferguson – the inventor and entrepreneur from Belfast who built a small, grey tractor which revolutionised the agricultural world. In particular, those who worked with him or knew him are afforded a special credibility within the organisation. These affectionate recollections are in stark contrast to the stories about the bankers in grey suits who nearly closed down the whole operation on a number of occasions in the 1970s and 1980s.

Symbols

Symbols are those things which support much of the culture in the organisation. Heavily symbolic items are often offices and office furniture, dining areas, cars, the order in which names appear on memos and so on. These symbols serve to emphasise the priorities and status (or lack of it) within the organisation. For example, a colleague of mine moved to another university and had innocently asked one of the site maintenance people if they could put another shelf in her office so she could cope with her large collection of books. This they duly did. She then found herself berated by her new colleagues as they all had just two shelves in their offices and only professors were entitled to three!

The language used can also be symbolic, and the language which is applied to customers can be particularly revealing. In one hospital trust, the general term for patients was 'trolley weights', and a railroad referred to its passengers as 'pedestrian freight'. The language and symbolism relating to customers is often far more powerful in driving the delivered strategy than any number of marketing plans or service initiatives

The mindset

The mindset or paradigm (the term used by Johnson[19]) is at the core of the culture and is therefore explained and supported by the aforementioned six elements. As a way of establishing the nature of the mindset, it is a valuable exercise to work through the six elements in order to clarify what the nature of the mindset is. Does the strategic customer profile prove to be a central element of the mindset? It is not sufficient just to put it in the middle, however – it needs to be supported by a number of elements in the six outer circles. This is how

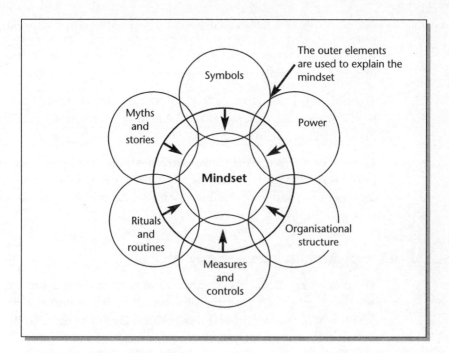

Figure 7.7 Creating the cultural web – the process of defining the mindset

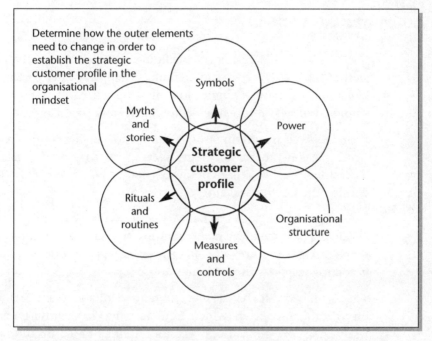

Figure 7.8 Rewebbing – identifying how the outer elements can create change in the mindset

we can in the first instance check whether or not the organisation is really being driven by a clear focus on its customers. If it is not, or if it is focused on the wrong types of customers, then the issue of customer-driven change needs to be considered.

The next stage, therefore, is to consider how the outer elements *should* look if the strategic customer profile is to be firmly established in the mindset of the organisation.

This process will identify the changes which may help to do this, but it may also identify the factors which are blocking this happening. These may be due to any of the mindsets in the lower part of Figure 7.2.

The customer-driven culture – an example

The following example is intended to illustrate how this process can be applied in an organisation. The example is a composite of a number of organisations and has been developed in order to illustrate the process. The key application of this process is, of course, to apply it to your own organisation.

Case study

CASE-RIGHT MANUFACTURING

Case-Right Manufacturing is a medium-sized operation in the north-west of the UK. The company manufactures heavy-duty packaging which has a variety of applications, but is particularly useful in the shipment of heavy or delicate components and products.

Increasingly, it is suffering from a number of smaller competitors which are consistently undercutting its prices. In addition, many of its customers are beginning to develop an in-house capability to develop their own packaging.

Historically, Case-Right has built its business on a customer base consisting of heavy-duty manufacturing companies, but, more and more, it seems that the role of high-technology businesses is becoming important to its future.

The incumbent MD has taken early retirement and a new MD is brought in by the shareholders from a totally different business sector. Figure 7.9 shows the cultural web for Case-Right Manufacturing at the point at which the new MD takes office.

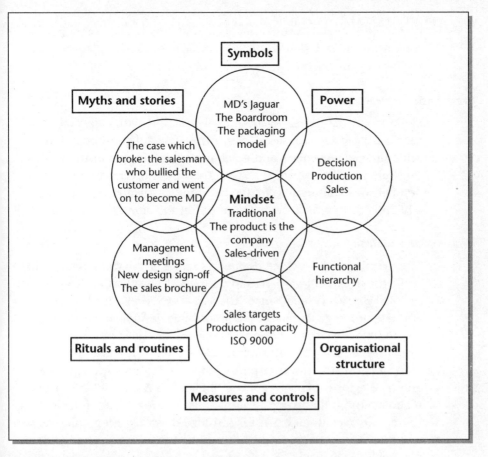

Figure 7.9 The cultural web for Case-Right Manufacturing

Power

The power within the organisation has traditionally been located in three of the main functions of the business – design, sales and production. As much of C-RM's work is of a bespoke nature, the design process is particularly important to the efficiency of the business. This also directly involves the sales function. The salesforce has a great deal of technical expertise and various of its members provide the design office with some very detailed specifications from which the designers develop the final design. Finally, production creates and installs the final packaging. This is a highly skilled operation and usually involves a number of changes in the final stages to ensure that the packaging allows the product to be loaded properly and safely. These three activities make up the central process of the organisation.

The reason for putting each of these areas in the power circle is that each is as powerful as the other and they dominate the workings of the organisation. Often conflicts between these three cause the overall running of the business to become dysfunctional.

Organisational structure

C-RM has a traditional organisational structure, with a general manager heading each department. These are design, production, sales, finance, personnel and purchasing. Within each of these areas there are middle managers, all with their own director to report to. Most of what happens is channelled through this formal structure, which tends to reflect the main groups in the organisation.

Measures and controls

The overall measure which dominates much of the thinking in C-RM is the use of sales targets. Within the sales department there are four regional managers reporting to the Sales Director. Each of these has an annual sales target based on the order value developed from the region. In addition, the regional managers also have notional responsibility for particular sectors. For example, the Regional Manager for the South is responsible for the high-technology sector and the Regional Manager for the Midlands is responsible for heavy manufacturing, the Export Regional Manager for the oil industry and so on. The overall sales target is cascaded down (by geographic region) and monthly meetings focus on the extent to which the annual sales plan will be achieved.

The sales department and the directors are paid on a bonus structure (as opposed to commission), which is based on the proportion of the annual sales plan they managed to achieve in terms of actual sales orders. The directors are also paid a bonus based on the efficiency of their own area in relation to the budgeted cost base. In the case of the production and design departments, this is expressed as a proportion of sales, while for the other functions it is expressed as a fixed figure agreed at the planning meeting in August. For the rest of the employees, a small bonus scheme exists which pays out when the sales target is achieved by 110 per cent. However, because of the intermittent nature of demand, at particular times of year the level of production capacity controls whether or not the direct workforce is earning increased sums through overtime or having to be placed on short-time work because demand is slack. The Production Director is concerned to maximise efficiency of the workforce.

Because many of C-RM's customers are supplying the military, it has to conform to BS 5750 or ISO 9000 standards. These standards require that systems and processes are traceable and require particular approaches to controlling and monitoring the various requests and design changes which occur in the system. The adoption of ISO 9000 is a relatively recent event and has required investment in both staff development and the types of systems employed by C-RM.

Rituals and routines

An important ritual at C-RM is the monthly management meeting. This is often a rather ill-tempered affair where blame is apportioned concerning the performance of the sales figures.

The main emphasis of the meeting is the detailed dissection of the order status report, which shows by region and industry type the orders which have been achieved and, more importantly, identifies the shortfall which needs to be met in order to keep the target on track. The outcome of this meeting – once the recriminations have stopped – is that the regional managers (the only managers below general management level who attend this meeting) berate their area managers who, in turn, then magically produce the orders they've kept up their sleeves after engaging in suitably loud and robust telephone conversations with their customers in order to pull the orders through.

Design sign-offs are also an important ritual and are often a key part of the monthly management meetings. Because of the potential liabilities if there was a failure in the packaging – both in terms of the customers' merchandise and the damage to carriers or other parties – the final design sign-off is made by the Managing Director, often after this has been discussed by the whole team.

While a lot of C-RM's sales are bespoke products, the Sales Director annually oversees the production of a sales brochure which identifies some of the 'off-the shelf' products which C-RM produces. These are items such as flight cases for electronics, musical instruments and other valuable items. The brochure includes details of the history of the organisation and shows some of the manufacturing approaches and design processes used by the company. The brochure is produced by an external design house, but involves a lot of deliberation on the part of the management team. Particular attention is paid to ensuring that the company's processes and design approaches are represented accurately.

Myths and stories

In the recent history of the organisation, the introduction of ISO 9000 has been a relatively successful innovation, which, despite some added bureaucracy, has been broadly supported. Part of the reason for its adoption was an event 15 years ago when a casing for a number of gas cannisters which had to be transported by air failed and caused an embarrassing and costly incident. The packaging which failed had been made from the wrong material, which has been specified by the customer and subsequently by the design group. For some reason, in production, the material used was porous rather than the impermeable standard specified by the design. As a small amount of seepage was expected from the gas cannisters, it was important that no moisture was allowed to enter the packing as this would cause a reaction which would significantly reduce the purity of the gas. Unfortunately, a high level of moisture *did* enter the packing and the gas, which was being shipped by air to the United States, arrived with a level of impurity which made it unacceptable for use by the customer. C-RM ended up having to fight an expensive law suit, which it subsequently lost. This story provided a powerful *raison d'être* for the introduction of ISO 9000 and it is still very much evident in the mindset of the top management team.

The other dominant story is that of the, now outgoing, MD. He had risen through the sales ranks to become MD and had held this position for the last 12 years. The story here reflects the ritual behaviour of the monthly meetings where the managers from sales ran out to the phones to bring in those critical orders to keep the budget on track, and it goes like this.

The MD is a rather large individual and the story goes that one big customer was proving particularly difficult to push into providing the commitment needed to fulfil the order target. Exasperated, in the large open-plan sales office, the MD allegedly boomed down the phone that if the customer did not commit there and then, he would personally come over and sit on his head until he agreed to do so. Allegedly the customer relented and committed to the order. The budget remained on track and the day was saved.

Symbols

Having been through the main elements of the culture of this organisation, it is probably relatively easy to predict what its dominant symbols are. As an engineering-based manufacturing company, the managerial and manual workforce are predominantly male. As often happens in such cultures, cars form an important symbolic part of status and position. First, all the cars have traditionally been British (not that this is possible any more!). The MD drives a Jaguar which is prominently parked in a dedicated position near the main entrance. The Design, Sales and Production Directors all have top-of-the-range Rovers. The general managers also have Rovers, but these are of a lower specification.

The general managers all have prominent offices in their areas of influence. The MD's office is next to the Boardroom where the monthly meetings take place. It is not possible to use this room for any other meeting other than the annual planning meetings in August. The Boardroom is decorated and furnished to a standard which is comparable only to the MD's office. An 'invitation' to present to the management group in the Boardroom is treated with great trepidation by other employees in the organisation.

The final symbol is the packaging itself. For a major contract to supply packaging for exploration equipment to the oil industry, a quarter-scale model was constructed as part of the bidding process. The order was won and the model returned. It is now proudly displayed on a plinth in the main reception area. A further model is also housed in a glass case in the Boardroom.

The mindset

Having worked through the six elements of the organisational culture, the mindset is the underlying set of values which drive the culture of the business. We are using these six areas to get at that which is never said or expressed but which clearly underlies the way in which the organisation operates.

The conclusion of this analysis is that the mindset is dominated by a number of core principles. The first of these is the process by which the product is created – the relationship between the original specification developed by the sales staff, the design process and the subsequent manufacture of the component. This process is unquestioned and assumed to be the basis on which the organisation must always operate, the assumption being that you cannot create an item of packaging unless you move through this process. This is supported by the clear focus on the three managers representing these activities as being the core power base of the organisation and the lessons learned from the failed gas canister packaging and the importance of supporting this process through ISO 9000.

The second aspect of the mindset is the sales process. The primary measures and controls of the organisation are all linked to the sales process, for both budgets and actual figures. The key question which the MD focuses on for most of the management meetings is sales levels relative to budget. This focus is accentuated by the reward systems and the relative status of the sales function in the organisation.

Finally, the culture of the organisation is one of tradition. The stories valued by the organisation all reflect enduring and sustaining qualities. The MD having been in place for 12 years, the only major change in recent times has been the adoption of a quality system (ISO 9000) which has simply reinforced the importance of the product creation process.

In defining the organisational mindset, it is also important to note what is absent as well as that which is present. In this case, there is a notable absence of a financial dimension, both in terms of the controls and measures (which are sales-driven) and the power structures of the organisation. One of the implications of the absence of financial emphasis, combined with the focus on the sales–design–production process, is that there may be cash-flow problems arising from a control system which is concerned with orders and a production process which involves a lengthy design stage. However, the main issue for the incoming MD is that the approach followed at C-RM is that there is no clear customer emphasis in the mindset of the organisation. In general, it seems to be more concerned with order levels than customer relationships and, where there is customer emphasis, this has tended to focus on the manufacturing sector when it is actually the high-technology sector that appears to be the strategic customer profile needed for the future.

Where does C-RM go from here?

Assuming that all this is the case, we now consider the rewebbing process which could be undertaken to build a customer focus and place the high-technology customers at the centre of the new web.

Power

While it is important not to undermine the excellence of the functional capabilities of C-RM, any customer-focused teams need to be more than nominal reporting lines. They should be given the resources and authority to emphasise that they are more than a notional concept. Before, the regional managers were given authority for particular

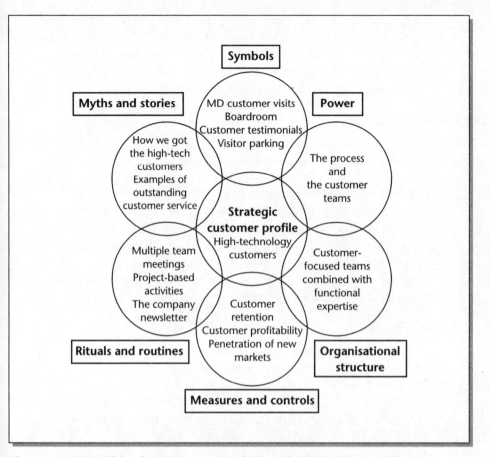

Figure 7.10 Rewebbing for C-RM – putting high-technology customers first

sectors, but all this meant was that they were praised if they were doing well or chastised if they were doing badly. In reality, they had no real influence over the performance of their allocated sector.

One way of achieving a shift in focus without encouraging too much direct opposition would be to appoint the more senior directors as chairs of these teams as this still shifts power to the team rather than the function.

Organisational structure

One of the first things which the new MD could do is to review the traditional structure and create a series of such customer-focused teams. These teams should be multidisciplinary and focus on particular customer profiles. If we assume that high-technology customers are the most important, we should put some of the most influential individuals into caring for this group. This would probably include the Sales Director and either the Production or Design Director. It is important that these teams are given appropriate authority which leads on to power.

Measures and controls

These are important changes. Historically, the process has been based on orders and how these will relate to the budget as well as the efficiency of the support functions. To move to customer profitability and retention levels presents some very real challenges to the information systems of C-RM. However, by initially reporting order levels and accounts receivable by customer group, this process can begin to develop. Other measures, such as relative satisfaction levels (an external agency could be used here), would begin to create a greater sense of the organisation's performance relative to different sectors and different customers.

Rituals and routines

While no MD wants to think that any new initiative will become ritualised, it is a powerful way of bedding down new approaches. In the new mindset it is important to move from a functional approach to that of a customer-focused team. Team meetings could become an important ritual, perhaps replacing the monthly sales meeting and with the MD attending the meetings of all the teams.

The team approach implies a greater emphasis on project management processes. At one level the production process has been closer to a form of project management than a mass-production process so this provides a basis on which to build. The notion that all main initiatives (such as a review of cash management) will be project-based is potentially a powerful way of building new thinking and ensuring that many of the valuable approaches to quality and process are not lost.

Finally, it is suggested that a company newsletter replaces the sales brochure. This would celebrate employees and their involvement in satisfying customers. It could also be used as a mechanism to make the organisation more transparent and accessible to all.

Myths and stories

This is probably the most difficult aspect to 'manage', but stories which emphasise the new mindset would be those which are concerned with customer relationships and extraordinary customer service. The only way in which these can be developed is for people to tell them. It is key that the MD has a number of influential allies in order to pass on such stories. However, there is a danger that if such stories are not true or are undermined in some way, they will become 'ironic' stories, serving to emphasise that such things never really work in practice, so they need to be handled with care.

Symbols

In order to emphasise the new approach, the Boardroom could be removed and rooms for team discussions be created. The old hierarchical approach can thus be replaced with a team-based approach.

The models of the packaging products could also be removed and replaced with customers' testimonials and examples of how customers' problems were quickly and efficiently solved, placing more emphasis on the people and the service than on the product.

The new MD could undertake a highly conspicuous series of customer visits with particular emphasis on the high-technology sector. A number of these customers could be invited to talk about their businesses and industries and the way they see things developing in the future.

The director's parking places could be removed so that they have to fight for a place like everyone else. These spaces could then be reserved for customers. A board could be installed in reception, welcoming customers and suppliers who visit the plant.

The new mindset

None of these changes, if implemented in isolation would make a difference, but together they begin to suggest a shift in the mindset which will build on the areas of excellence in the organisation and, further, open the company up so it can respond to these developing opportunities. One of the ways in which this process can be formulated is to identify the factors which will facilitate a shift towards satisfying a new customer group and those which may create barriers to this change. A 'forcefield analysis'[20] is one technique which can be used to do this by isolating the key factors which need to be addressed in managing a change. This is illustrated in Figure 7.11.

In this example, the need for change to a new customer focus is being assisted by concern about the financial performance of the organisation, the desire for change on the part of younger members of the management team and the arrival of a new MD. However, the forces which are constraining the ability to change are the more

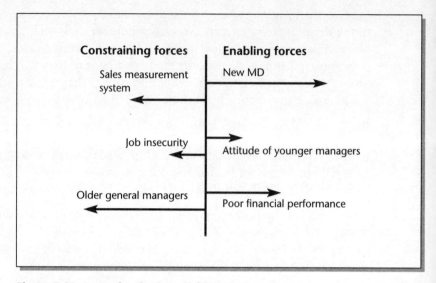

Figure 7.11 Example of a forcefield analysis

conservative general managers, a concern about job security, which is making it difficult for individuals to believe that changing some of their behaviours and responsibilities is going to be to their benefit in the long run, and the measurement system for the salesforce's performance, which is well established and encourages a particular type of behaviour.

This chapter has sought to raise our understanding as to how an organisation may really become customer focused. However, it is important to recognise that is is questionable as to whether issues such as organisational mindset and customer focused change can really be 'managed'. The underlying message is that simply demanding or exhorting organisational members to become more customer focused is at best inadequate, at worst will create exactly the opposite behaviours to those intended. Real change comes from change in the embedded nature of what the organisation, and the individuals within it are about. It is only when the day-to-day routines of the business start with the customer that it can begin to claim to be truly customer focused.

KEY SUMMARY POINTS

1 The organisational mindset is the basis on which the organisation will or will not be able to deliver a customer-focused strategy. This mindset can be a powerful basis for sustaining the strategy, but it can also be a major obstacle to its achievement.

2 The alignment between the mindset and the environment can be seen at four different levels:
- internal
- external, non-customer
- yesterday's customers
- the strategic customer groups mindset.

The last mindset represents alignment between the organisation and its customers whereas the first three imply a lack of such alignment.

3 Individual mindsets regarding customers can be defined by means of customer stereotypes. These represent the way in which customers are viewed and, therefore, the way in which these customers are expected to respond to changes in value and price.

4 Mindsets are supported and reinforced by the culture of the organisation.

5 The cultural web provides a way of clarifying the nature of the mindset of an organisation. It is based on an understanding of the six elements of an organisation's culture:
- power
- organisational structure
- measures and controls
- rituals and routines
- myths and stories
- symbols.

6 In order to develop a mindset which is aligned to the strategic customer profile, we need to adapt the six outer elements of the cultural web in such a way that they help create and sustain the change.

7 Forcefield analysis is a useful way in which to identify the key factors in the organisational culture which will assist or block attempts to move towards focusing on a particular type of customer profile.

KEY QUESTIONS AND DIAGNOSTICS

Can you identify which is your company's mindset from among the four outlined in Figure 7.2?

In considering the cultural web of your organisation, what conclusions can you draw about the mindset which underlies the way in which the organisation sees its customers?

Write down the three most important enablers which you think will help generate greater focus on customers in the organisation. Then write down the three most important constraints. What do you conclude from this?

STRATEGIC THINKING DIAGNOSTIC

Score each of these statements in terms of how strongly you agree or disagree with them. Add up the scores and see what your total means.

	Agree			Disagree	
Our mindset is one which completely ignores customers.	1	2	3	4	5
While we were very customer-focused once, this is now no longer the case.	1	2	3	4	5
While we claim to be customer-focused, all the internal dialogue is about the provision of products and services, not customers.	1	2	3	4	5
Our mindset has been fixed for the last ten years and you are not going to be able to change it now.	1	2	3	4	5
We are very adaptable and are continually redefining our mindset to fit with the customers' environment.	5	4	3	2	1
We are into a very well-established routine and do not want to rock the boat.	1	2	3	4	5
Culture is something for the human resources people to worry about – we just get on with selling the products.	1	2	3	4	5

Score

25–35: All the indications are that a customer-focused mindset exists in your company.

15–25: Some positive indicators, but how do they compare with the competition? Would they be scoring higher?

0–15: This indicates that there is very little focus on the customer in your organisation.

SUGGESTED FURTHER READING

Vandermerwe, S. (1995), 'The Process of Market-driven Transformation', *Long Range Planning*, **28**, 2, 79–91

Johnson, G. (1992), 'Managing Strategic Change – Strategy, Culture and Action', *Long Range Planning*, **25**, 1, 28–36

REFERENCES

[1] Johnson, G. (1992), 'Managing Strategic Change – Strategy, Culture and Action', *Long Range Planning*, **25**, 1, 28–36

[2] For example, Pettigrew, A, and Whipp, R. (1991), *Managing Change for Competitive Success*, Oxford, Basil Blackwell, and Schein, E. H. (1986). *Organizational Culture and Leadership*, SF Jossey Bass

[3] A notable exception is the work of Sandra Vandermerwe – for example, 'The Process of Market-driven Transformation', *Long Range Planning*, **28**, 2, 79–91

[4] Spender, J.-C. (1989), *Industry Recipes: The Nature and Sources of Management Judgement*, Oxford, Basil Blackwell

[5] Smith, K. G., Grimm, C. M., Gannon, M. J., and Chen, M. (1991), 'Organizational Information Processing, Competitive Responses and Performance in the US Domestic Airline Industry', *Academy of Management Journal*, **34**, 60–85

[6] Prahalad, C. K., and Bettis, R. A. (1986), 'The Dominant Logic: A New Linkage Between Diversity and Performance', *Strategic Management Journal*, **7**, 485–501

[7] See, for example, Levitt, T. (1960), 'Marketing Myopia', *Harvard Business Review*, July–August, 45–56

[8] Narver, J. C., and Slater, S. F. (1990), 'The Effect of a Market Orientation on Business Profitability', *Journal of Marketing*, **54**, October, 20–35

[9] Kohil, A. K., and Jaworski, B. J. (1990), 'Market Orientation: The Construct, Research Propositions, and Managerial Implications, *Journal of Marketing*, **54**, 1–18

[10] Day, G. S., and Nedungadi, P. (1994), 'Managerial Representations of Competitive Positioning', *Journal of Marketing*, **58**, April, 31–44

[11] Mintzberg, H., and Waters, J. A. (1985), 'Of Strategies, Deliberate and Emergent', *Strategic Management Journal*, 6, **3**, 257–72

[12] See Augoustinos, M., and Walker, I. (1995), *Social Cognition: An Integrated Introduction*, London, Sage, for an overview of the work on social stereotypes

[13] Katz, D., and Brady, K. (1933), 'Racial Stereotypes in One Hundred College Students', *Journal of Abnormal and Social Psychology*, **28**, 280–90

[14] Rosenkrantz, P., Vogel, S., Bee, Broverman, I., and Broverman, D. M. (1968), 'Sex Role Stereotypes and Self-concepts in College Students', *Journal of Consulting and Clinical Psychology*, **32**, 3, 287–95

[15] ibid.

[16] The framework outlined by Johnson uses the term 'paradigm' at its centre. I, however, have used the term 'mindset' to represent the overarching way in which the organisation responds to the environment.

[17] Jenkins, M., and McDonald, M. H. B. (1997), 'Defining and Segmenting Markets: Archetypes and Research Agendas', *European Journal of Marketing*, **31**, 1, 9–24

[18] See KPMG case study in Johnson, G., and Scholes, K. (1993), *Exploring Corporate Strategy*, (3rd ed.) Hemel Hempstead, Prentice-Hall

[19] ibid.

[20] See Grundy, T. (1994), *Strategic Learning in Action*, Maidenhead, McGraw-Hill, for a description of forcefield analysis

PART 3

REFLECTIONS
AND ACTIONS

CHAPTER

8

REFLECTIONS ON
THE PROCESS

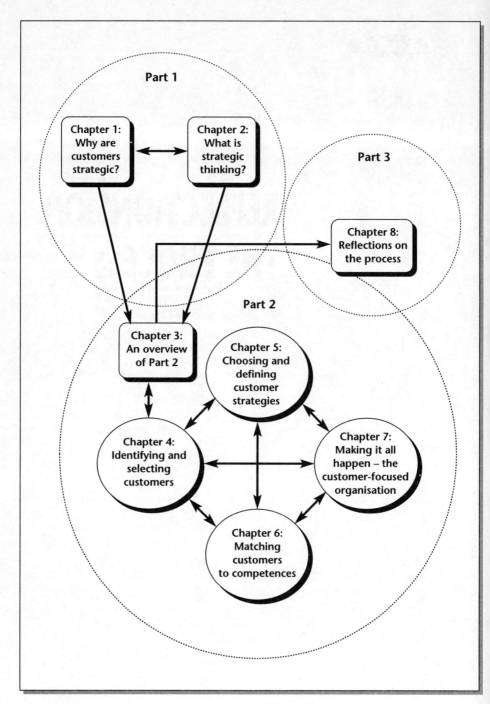

Figure 8.1 Overview map of the book

In this final chapter, we reflect on the issues which have been raised and the ground covered. First, we shall review the previous sections and, then, we shall look at some case studies which bring out the issues raised throughout the book.

Figure 8.1 is an overview of the book. Figure 8.1 shows the three distinct parts – Part 1 providing the rationale for the book, Part 2 the iterative model for developing thinking about customers and Part 3 reflecting on the process.

In order to revisit and reflect on the issues raised in the subsequent sections, we use a series of questions that are designed to explore how the framework can be used.

Are these issues relevant to public-sector organisations?

Because public-sector organisations are often dealing with multiple and diverse customer groups and stakeholders, it is particularly important that these different groups are surfaced and discussed in the organisation. The danger of the whole 'customer focus' issue is that, because of multiple customer definitions, there is still a lot of confusion and inconsistency in public-sector organisations.

The frameworks outlined in the previous chapters provide a basis for surfacing and discussing who these different customer groups are and why they are important to the organisation.

Are the frameworks specific to business units or are there corporate- and functional-level applications?

The way in which these ideas have been applied in the book has been to focus at the business unit-level, where the concerns of customer direction, focus and position are central to the development of the business unit. However, these concepts can be applied equally well at the corporate level. For example, the customer growth matrix (Figure 5.3), can be used to develop the logic of corporate diversification through acquisition – are we extending the businesses that supply to our existing customers or are we acquiring new groups of customers from similar businesses? These questions also relate to where synergy can be achieved by serving customers better by either adding value or enhancing cost. For example, in the case of a food company which is vertically integrated as a result of corporate acquisitions, it can claim to have greater control over the supply chain, thereby reducing the likelihood of disease. In this case, a particular collection of business units adds value to the customer at the end of the supply chain.

Similarly, these frameworks can be used to explore the issues facing particular functional groups within the organisation. For example, the transport department of a manufacturing firm would benefit from isolating out who its key customer groups are and determining where it needs to place emphasis in the future. The question here is where do particular functions add value or bring efficiencies to the way in which we deal with particular customer groups?

If everyone reads this book we will not be any further forward will we?

While the concepts and processes may be the same for everyone, each organisation and its context is uniquely to them. Therefore, the ways in which these ideas will be applied will be different for each organisation and will be more successful in some organisations than others.

It all seems a lot of work, and it is very difficult to see where the benefits will be

The value of this process is the questions it suggests. It is not intended that every reader should work blindly through every set of issues, but, rather, that you can pick up certain parts of the model and explore them at certain times as appropriate.

CASE STUDIES

The purpose of these case studies is to relate the issues covered in the book to particular organisational contexts. Each case is based on a fictitious organisation, although it is intended that the description should be familiar to those working in these types of organisations. They are not intended to provide examples of good or bad practices, but simply to illuminate and explore the issues raised in earlier chapters.

Each case is followed by a brief analysis, which suggests where some of the critical issues for the development of the organisation may lie.

THE COMPONENTS MANUFACTURER

This organisation has a long history of manufacturing which originated in the late nineteenth century. The organisation successfully expanded its operations in the 1970s and 1980s by means of agents and third-party agreements across the world. However, its culture is largely parochial and has tended to be largely production-led. The company struggled through the recessionary period of the 1980s, largely as a result of the loyalty of a number of its large customers. However, in recent times, these customers have been purchased by international holding companies and have developed centralised purchasing policies which has meant that the organisation has lost a number of its long-standing customers. The customer base is relatively polarised, with smaller, local customers providing around 20 per cent of the organisation's revenues, but these customers are often distributors or sub-assemblers of components and are therefore in a very similar position to this organisation. The larger customers are the manufacturers which are buying in a variety of components from around the world

The organisation has managed to successfully develop its manufacturing and production processes in order to keep in line with the many quality initiatives, such as ISO 9000. Its production operation is now much leaner than it was five years ago and it has invested in new technology in order to manage its inbound logistics and operations.

Despite these developments, there are still some issues the organisation is trying to respond to. One of these is the increasing pressure from its customers to restrict the number of suppliers they deal with and to only use organisations with which they feel they can develop a long-term relationship so they can enhance their efficiency and effectiveness in the marketplace. The other is an increased desire on the part of its customers for more of the assembly work to be completed by their suppliers. In other words, rather than buying in castings, seals and filters separately, they are now looking to source the entire item. This creates an opportunity for added value business, but it also means that the production capabilities of the organisation need to be continually expanded. The components made by this company are an established brand and are well recognised by their customers' customer, although they would not be influential in the final decision to purchase.

Most of the competition experienced by this company is from international organisations located elsewhere in Europe and in the Far East. While its customers consider the organisation easy to do business with and particularly flexible and responsive, the decision as to which suppliers to use is increasingly being made not by its customers but by their head offices in the USA or France or Germany.

It seems that a number of strategic decisions need to be made in terms of which are its priority customers and, therefore, the type of organisation it needs to become.

Some observations

The key issue facing this organisation seems to be that of choosing which customer groups it builds the strategy around (the evaluation process outlined in Table 4.2, for example, could be used to clarify which groups the organisation should focus on). It seems a relatively clear-cut conclusion that, for the organisation to continue to be viable, it needs to focus on making the larger manufacturers its primary customer base. The small customers, while perhaps fitting more closely with where the organisation is now, appear to be unlikely to survive in their current form. It seems that the pressures in the environment will tend to drive further consolidation, both vertically along the supply chain – with suppliers increasing their abilities to produce sub-assemblies rather than just separate components – and horizontally – with competitors merging and making acquisitions.

The competences of the organisation appear to centre on its production processes and the quality of the products it produces. The challenge is to maintain these and become an organisation which can deal with the changes occurring in its large, global customers, which will require long-term commitment rather than short-term responses (see Table 6.1 for a framework for linking competences to customers). These changes require a further shift away from the largely internal mindset the organisation has at present to one which is focused on these large organisations and developing the competences required to build on and sustain these particular types of relationships (the issues of identifying and managing change in the organisational mindset are summarised by means of the worked example shown in Figure 7.10).

THE HOSPITAL

The hospital trust is a creation of new legislation in the UK which has sought to create something like a free market, moving away from the traditional values of the National Health Service.

The general mindset of the hospital we shall look at here is that medical values are central to its existence and that those who provide this medical expertise know best. The ethos is that the hospital exists to allow medical expertise to be applied, which is distinct from meeting the needs of particular patients. The power tends to lie with the clinicians rather than the management of the hospital.

The changes that have been made to the way in which the provision of healthcare is delivered have required that the organisation change the way it sees the outside world. Whether or not the term 'customer' is appropriate here, hospitals have had to come to terms with the notion of responding to multiple stakeholders, such as patients, doctors and local authorities, each of these groups having their own requirements and perspectives and each bringing different challenges to the way in which the organisation may respond. Undoubtedly the staff throughout the hospital, whether they be nurses, consultants or porters, play a key role in this process and have different views as to which are the key customer groups and respond accordingly.

Some observations

This case is one which is particularly difficult and problematical because of the complicated and embedded way in which the hospital works. It would be overly simplistic to suggest that what is needed is a clear focus on a particular customer group. However, it is important that some overall strategic customer profiles (see Figure 5.6) are developed in order to provide a basis for discussion so that it is then possible to build some coherence into the overall direction the organisation is taking.

The fundamental problem is one of multiple and conflicting mindsets, all of which are relatively myopic and resistant to divergent possibilities (see

Figure 2.3 for an illustration of the difference between these modes of seeing and interpreting things). However, these problems are not unique to hospitals, though they will be exaggerated in this case, given a lack of overall direction.

In Chapter 2, the example of the myopia needed in order to develop an overall focus is relevant here. However, the problem with achieving myopia is that it does require an undisputed source so that we can get on with following the direction of the organisation rather than questioning the source of the myopia. In this situation, continued movement around the model outlined in Figure 3.1 will begin to raise some of the central issues which need to be dealt with by the organisation as a whole, though this will be a complicated, messy and challenging task.

Case study

THE CONSTRUCTION COMPANY

The construction industry has passed through a number of major transitions in recent years. It is still a relatively fragmented industry, made up of some national providers with recognised names and many thousands of smaller, independent organisations which operate within complicated networks, coming together to work on particular projects and then dissipating to form new alliances for new projects.

The focus of this case is a medium-sized organisation which operates in a relatively rural region in the east of the UK. This organisation is well known in the area and has traditionally undertaken small-scale projects, such as road repairs, pavement construction and the laying of cables and pipes. Recently, the deregulation of the major energy utilities and the growth in the telecommunications industry have meant that there has been a huge increase in pipe and cable laying and maintenance work. This has meant that the organisation has grown significantly in recent years and taken on a relatively new management team with the single objective of sustaining this rate of growth in order that the company may be floated on the stock market within the next five years.

However, this growth is threatened by the increase in competition which the booming market in cable laying has created. Also a number of acquisitions in the utilities market have meant that the holding companies (which in this region are predominately French) are seeking to improve the efficiency of their acquisitions by using their own, in-house construction capabilities. They also see the construction and maintenance aspects of the business becoming major sources of profit in the future.

The company is therefore seeking to significantly grow their activities in this increasingly competitive situation. The organisation's competences are based on the wide range of activities which they can take on at any one time – from laying electrical cables to building bridges. They are therefore positioning themselves as form of regional 'one-stop shop' for construction work.

Some observations

It seems that this organisation still has a number of choices in terms of where it positions itself on the customer growth matrix (see Figure 5.3). It is likely that there is a great deal of loyalty to the company by its existing customers and therefore strategies which extend the services being offered to these customers or acquire customers on the basis of this loyalty are some of the options which need to be considered. It is also likely that the application of scenarios (see Chapter 4) may suggest some further issues worthy of exploration. For example, the possibility of merging with similar construction companies in other regions in order or provide a comprehensive service targeted specifically at the utility companies. Further, the environmental issues relating to this work suggest that things will become considerably tougher, so it is important to consider a range of potential responses to these at this point.

se study

THE FOOD MANUFACTURER

This organisation produces a number of food items based on its original business, which was that of a potato merchant. The organisation now makes frozen chips and other potato products, including powdered potato, which is primarily used by other food manufacturers as an ingredient in their products, and also chilled, prepared products such as potato waffles.

The channels the organisation operates in are therefore relatively complicated and, while it has a good idea who its immediate customers are, it knows relatively little about the ways in which its products are ultimately consumed.

Like most food manufacturers, the organisation is under continued pressure from the multiple retailers, both to reduce its prices and to provide higher levels of added value by means of innovation and enhanced product formulations. All of this has squeezed margins and the organisation has been considering whether or not there are any realistic alternatives to its current ongoing strategy of fighting for space on the retailers' shelves. The views of the salesforce and the Sales Director are clear – this is the only way in which the company is going to make the tough targets set by the holding company. This strategy requires high-pressure selling, using the relationships with the retail buyers in order to keep building up the orders and achieve the revenue levels needed to meet the targets.

However, there seems to be some interest developing in a new process for creating a high-quality mashed potato product from powder. One of the general managers has had some preliminary discussions with a number of food services companies, including two well-known burger chains which are considering using it for some fried potato products on their new breakfast menus. The General Manager believes that it is time to build a new part of the business which does not involve the huge pressures which the retail businesses exert on the organisation.

Some observations

This situation is one in which there are tensions between today's strategic customer profile and the profile needed to ensure the continued growth of the organisation. Referring to the customer growth matrix (see Figure 5.3), it can be seen that there are some fundamental tensions between continuing to build business with the multiple retailers and shifting emphasis to food services customers where new and attractive opportunities beckon.

Scenario analysis (see Chapter 4) would be useful here as a means of exploring some of the possibilities. It would also point up the fact that the food service sector is a new opportunity but this does not mean that it is also free from all the threats and constraints which exist with multiple retailers.

It can also be seen that there are some cultural issues underpinning this debate about the organisation's future. The Sales Director and her team have probably based their expertise and careers on working with multiple retailer buyers, so to expect them to suddenly switch from the environment they know so well to a new one is unrealistic. Similarly, it seems that the General Manager is staking his hopes on this new customer group. This provides him with some positive energy, but it may also produce certain counter-responses to other ideas and may lead to the myopia outlined in Chapter 2 and the failure of this initiative being seen as the failure of this individual's attempts to make a name for himself.

THE BUSINESS SCHOOL

A business school is there to deliver management education by means of individual tutors who give lecturers, readings and seminar work. The main elements of the business school are its academic staff, who deliver the content and processes of management education, the administrative support network and the facilities of the school.

The customer groups it serves are very wide and dispersed, but they can be summarised as being organisations, in a wide range of sectors, both private and public, both small and local and large and global. These organisations tend to develop ongoing relationships with the business school, but are often in the process of change and reorientation. In addition to organisations, the school's customers are also individuals. They can be from a wide variety of circumstances. They can be building a route for themselves up through the organisation employing them or in a state of redeployment, where their existing career path has come to a stop and they are seeking to reorient themselves in some particular direction.

The needs of organisations are those of becoming better able deal with their environments, which may be achieved by increasing their effectiveness and efficiency by developing their staff. They may also be seeking to encourage strategic thinking and enhance creativity and problem solving by being provided with systematic tools and frameworks they can use to achieve these ends.

For individuals, there are various factors at work, including the need for credibility with their peers and wanting to undertake a particular course because they assume they will become more effective, which will ultimately lead to increased promotion opportunities, job satisfaction and security. Also they may be wanting a change in direction or orientation, reskilling themselves for a general management career path.

While this particular business school has traditionally relied on a large number of public or open programmes which are attended by managers from a wide variety of organisations, both large and small, in a wide variety of sectors, from shipping to financial services, from computer software to aerospace, the new Director of the school believes that there is a new phase in business education developing which is built on the provision of company-specific programmes. In order to follow up this belief, he creates the position of a director responsible for the development of in-company programmes and encourages all the current course directors to use the designs of their existing courses to deliver company-specific programmes.

Some observations

This case illustrates the situation where a switch is being made between an emphasis on one customer group (principally the individual, short-course delegate) and another (organisations and those responsible for overall training and development). What is important here is to recognise that this switch has significant implications for the internal workings of the organisation. It is not simply a question of redirecting the marketing efforts of the business school. The move raises a set of questions concerning the internal mindset and how it aligns with this new focus.

It is likely that the course directors who have well-established public courses which they know work well will be reluctant to simply offer these as in-company programmes. Because of the diverse nature of management groups, it is likely that such courses are designed around particular case studies. This design is largely inappropriate for in-company programmes as the delegates and sponsors will be seeking real organisational outcomes from the course. In addition, the actual process of an in-company programme is fundamentally different as a great deal of time and effort needs to be spent at the beginning, defining the objectives and methods of delivery. With the current open programmes, however, all of this work has already been done and so staff can simply concentrate on delivering the programme rather than having to go through lengthy deliberations on design.

All of these factors suggest that, despite the fact that a decision has been made to switch emphasis to a different customer group, these other factors, which need to be taken into account in order to deliver this in the organisation, have not really been noticed. This strategy is therefore in danger of not being realised while the realised strategy is being driven by everyone behaving in the same way as they always have (see Figure 7.4).

PRO-FORMA FOR APPLYING TO YOUR ORGANISATION

Framework 1
Identifying the customer groups you serve

Customer groups and contexts	Provide revenue	Make decision	Benefit from product
1			
2			
3			
4			
5			
6			
7			

Framework 2
Identifying strategically important customers now and in the future

	Customer 1		Customer 2	
	Now	Future	New	Future
Size of business				
Influence over other customers				
Stability				
Lack of competition				
Opportunity to offer added value				
Opportunity to save costs				
Totals				

Framework 3
Scenario development: identifying the certain driving forces

Certain (forces for change)	
Driving force	Outcome

Framework 4
Scenario development: identifying the uncertain driving forces

Uncertain (forces for change)			
Driving force	Outcome 1	Outcome 2	Rank

Framework 5
Onion diagram for plotting outcomes of uncertain forces

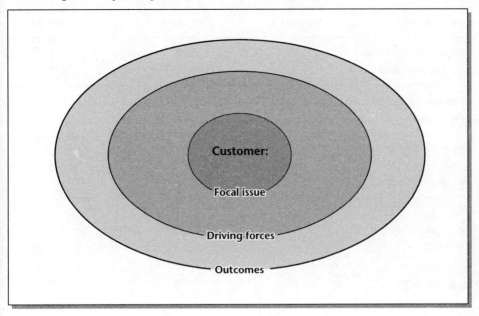

Framework 6
Assessment of the impact of a scenario

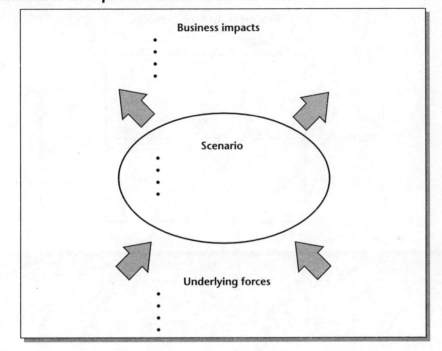

Framework 7
Exploring the impacts of different scenarios

Implications	Scenario 1	Scenario 2	Scenario 3
Signals expected in the environment			
Possible seed-setting activities			
Strengths and weaknesses of all competitors			
Strategy evaluation			

Framework 8
The customer growth matrix

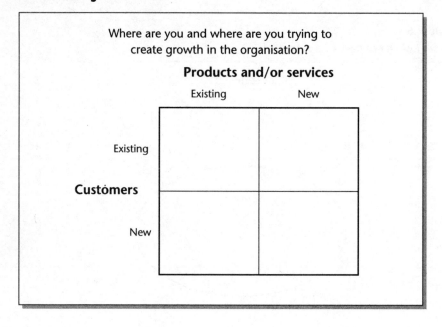

Where are you and where are you trying to create growth in the organisation?

Products and/or services

Existing   New

Existing

Customers

New

Framework 9
Outlining the strategic customer profile

Strategic customer profile: Customer 1	
Characteristics	
Context	

Framework 10
Plotting your position on the customer matrix

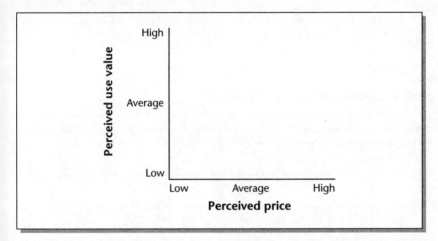

Framework 11
Identifying and weighting the dimensions of PUV and price

PUV dimensions	Weight	Product A		Product B		Product C	
		Rating	Score	Rating	Score	Rating	Score
1							
2							
3							
4							
5							
Total							
Price							

Framework 12
Matching PUV dimensions and price to competences

PUV dimensions	Competences	Competence	Rarity	Sustainability
Price dimension				
Competence score				
Sustained advantage score				

Framework 13
Identifying opportunities for building sustainable competitive advantage

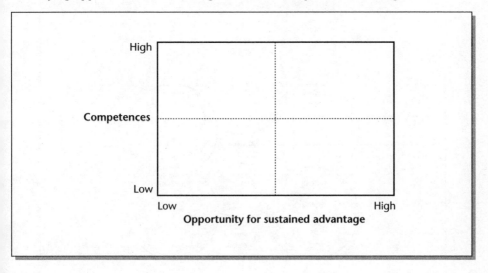

Framework 14
Plotting customer stereotypes (for business customers)

Small	1	2	3	4	5	6	7	Large
Slow	1	2	3	4	5	6	7	Fast
Variable	1	2	3	4	5	6	7	Consistent
Co-operative	1	2	3	4	5	6	7	Arrogant
Frugal	1	2	3	4	5	6	7	Generous
Undemanding	1	2	3	4	5	6	7	Demanding
Promiscuous	1	2	3	4	5	6	7	Loyal
Struggling	1	2	3	4	5	6	7	Successful
Traditional	1	2	3	4	5	6	7	Radical
Flexible	1	2	3	4	5	6	7	Rigid
Local	1	2	3	4	5	6	7	Global
Cost driven	1	2	3	4	5	6	7	Performance-driven
Old	1	2	3	4	5	6	7	Young
Prevaricating	1	2	3	4	5	6	7	Decisive
Specialist	1	2	3	4	5	6	7	Generalist
Reactive	1	2	3	4	5	6	7	Proactive
Distant	1	2	3	4	5	6	7	Involved
Inward-looking	1	2	3	4	5	6	7	Outward-looking

Framework 15
The culture web of an organisation

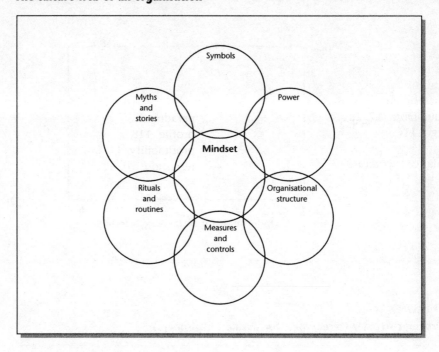

Framework 16
Forcefield analysis

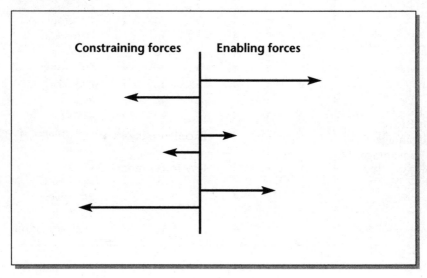

INDEX